VOTE
WITH
YOUR
PHONE

VOTE WITH YOUR PHONE

Why Mobile Voting Is Our Final Shot at Saving Democracy

BRADLEY TUSK

This publication is designed to provide accurate and authoritative information in regard to the subject matter covered. It is sold with the understanding that the publisher is not engaged in rendering legal, accounting, or other professional service. If legal advice or other expert assistance is required, the services of a competent professional person should be sought.—*From a Declaration of Principles Jointly Adopted by a Committee of the American Bar Association and a Committee of Publishers and Associations*

This book is not intended as a substitute for medical advice from a qualified physician. The intent of this book is to provide accurate general information in regard to the subject matter covered. If medical advice or other expert help is needed, the services of an appropriate medical professional should be sought.

Published by Sourcebooks
P.O. Box 4410, Naperville, Illinois 60567-4410
(630) 961-3900
sourcebooks.com

Cataloging-in-Publication Data is on file with the Library of Congress.

Printed and bound in the United States of America
LSC 10 9 8 7 6 5 4 3 2 1

For Abby and Lyle
For Laurel

CONTENTS

....

PART 4: PERSONAL ESSAYS
(THE PEOPLE WHO LIKE MOBILE VOTING)

PART 5: WHAT YOU CAN DO ABOUT IT

FOREWORD

A fter the shooting at my high school in Parkland, Florida, I was fucking enraged. I had learned in debate about gun policy and had to argue on both sides of the issue. I know that the reason the shooting happened was because of our corrupt system of government that legalized bribery via campaign donations by groups like the National Rifle Association (NRA). I was mad after the shooting, because I felt guilty knowing that I could have been advocating long before for the policies I know could have prevented it and also the epic failure of our leaders to do anything about gun violence. I remember thinking in middle school when I saw the news about Sandy Hook that something had to change, but it didn't.

Now in Florida, many thought we couldn't change anything because we were teenagers and Florida was a Republican state, but we didn't listen and still tried. From that day until now, I know the number one thing we could do to prevent gun violence is make our democracy as accessible as possible because the *vast* majority of the

American people, including Floridians, support stronger gun laws, but a loud and immoral minority that is the gun lobby has subverted the people's will.

What got us through it was an outpouring of love and support from our families and our community—and the support of millions upon millions of people from across the country and the world.

Our pain connected with people across the world, and a new chapter of the movement to end gun violence was born from that connection. My classmates and I became the leaders of that new chapter. In the whirlwind of activism that followed the shooting, nearly two million people marched with us in Washington, DC, and around the country.

How did a group of high school activists—without connections, experience, money, or power—become the leaders of a movement that would shake the halls of Congress?

What made the difference for us?

Our phones.

The school-shooting generation was just barely old enough to speak out, but Gen Z is the most connected generation in history. We grew up with phones that connected us to each other and to the older generations directly and personally. A new movement was born, in Facebook groups and Twitter conversations, on Instagram and TikTok.

Maybe we shouldn't have been surprised; after all, people of all ages have been talking, texting, emailing, banking, grocery shopping, dating, and more on their phones for years. It's not just Gen Z. Practically everyone trusts their phones to connect them safely and securely to the world.

It's time for the digital revolution to continue to level the playing field and expand our democracy. Hundreds of millions of people communicate, organize, and conduct financial transactions on their phones.

Now, it's time to have voting on our phones as an option.

Mobile voting could be a catalyst for creating a democracy where voting is accessible and inclusive and keeping up with the technology of our generation. In the 2020 election, about eighty million eligible voters didn't cast their vote. This was an election with the highest turnout since 1900, yet millions remained unheard. Imagine a democracy where the voting booth is at the fingertips of every eligible voter, a democracy where everyday Americans are unburdened by the limitations of physical polling stations and long lines.

Right now, voting just isn't accessible. As voting currently stands, the challenges of accessibility are painfully evident. Americans in every city and state experience the taxing struggle of balancing work shifts and long waits to exercise their democratic right to vote, and young voters are particularly impacted.

The impact of mobile voting on voter turnout would be revolutionary. We're talking about a world where casting your vote is as simple as sending a text. If your polling site is in your pocket, the inconveniences of going to vote disappear. It turns the act of voting into a seamless part of our day, increasing the participation of every citizen, especially young people, in shaping the policies and leadership of our nation.

But we're not just going to adapt to the status quo. We're changing it. Automatic voter registration is happening across the country and the world, and it's about time. Here in the United States, states like Pennsylvania—which in September 2023 implemented automatic voter registration when a resident gets their driver's license—are setting a precedent for how we can expand our democratic system and make voting more accessible.

If the government has the ability to send draft cards when you turn eighteen and securely maintains the tax information of every citizen, automatic voter registration should be a given in our modern society. The discrepancy between our technological progress and our outdated voting system is a glaring contradiction we cannot afford to ignore.

We live in an era dominated by technology, from organizing marches to handling our finances. If banking systems, which deal with our economic lifelines, can be securely operated via our cell phones, the prospect of mobile voting becomes not just plausible but imperative. If our actions can be securely authenticated for sensitive transactions, there's no conceivable reason why our votes can't be similarly safeguarded.

The security concerns surrounding mobile voting are important, and we should only implement such a system if we can guarantee it's secure. What is clear is that if we built it securely, mobile voting can be as secure and as convenient as everyday online activities such as online banking, healthcare, and transportation.

Testing grounds for mobile voting in seven states have already demonstrated its feasibility, with people with disabilities and the military using this system successfully. The realization of an end-to-end verifiable mobile voting technology, available freely to any jurisdiction, is within our grasp. We are at a pivotal point, with outdated excuses becoming intolerable. We need to unite our voices for a democracy that genuinely mirrors the technological advances our society has made.

Plus, this isn't a battle between Democrats and Republicans; it's about reshaping a democracy where every voice counts. It's about communities everywhere having equal say in who represents us and what policies are prioritized. It's about a leveled playing field where every vote has equal weight, and gerrymandering doesn't get the final say. Mobile voting will also revolutionize access to the ballot for rural communities and working people, irrespective of one's political affiliation, reducing travel constraints and promoting universal participation. The objective is simple: to create a system where the best argument wins, not whoever has the most convenient voting location.

As Gen Z, we need to debunk stereotypes about our political apathy and address the reluctance to adapt our systems. Youth turnout in recent elections has already broken records. Now, our call for change is a collective desire for a fairer and more representative political landscape. It's time to break free from outdated systems and embrace the digital era.

The future of politics can be a realm where every voice is heard, every vote is counted, and every individual matters.

In 2018, after the deadly massacre at my high school that changed so many lives forever, I knew that the only thing I could do was scare the fuck out of the corrupt politicians on the left and right who failed for decades to act on gun violence. I knew that we had to stand up against the gun lobby and vote NRA puppets, whether left or right, out of office. (Sad but true, there were and are still some on the left.) While we've been marching and mobilizing for the last five years, we also have the power and technology to create something that will ensure every person can do the one thing that makes a difference: vote. I know from my experience that the only good politician is a scared one. The best way to bring our democracy back from the brink is to make it as accessible as possible to the American people through systems like mobile voting and automatic voter registration so the only special interest politicians care about is the people's interest.

By embracing mobile voting, we are not just advocating for technological advancement; we are fortifying our commitment to a democracy that is of the people, by the people, and for the people. Mobile voting is not a distant dream; it's an attainable reality and it's not going away.

David Hogg
Co-Founder and president—**Leaders We Deserve**
Co-Founder and board member—**March for Our Lives**

PART 1

THE SYSTEM IS VERY, VERY BROKEN

CHAPTER 1

WHY THINGS FEEL SO BAD

(And What We Can Do about It)

f you're reading this book, you're probably pretty up to speed with the state of the world. And anyone up to speed with the state of the world probably feels screwed. I don't blame you. Everything feels terrible right now. Climate change is causing massive upheaval everywhere. Mass shootings keep happening over and over again—and no one does anything about it. Our schools aren't preparing kids adequately for college or the workforce. Our healthcare system is wildly expensive, while millions still lack basic coverage. We have no idea what to do with the influx of migrants crossing the border—we don't know to stop them from entering the country or what to do with them once they're here.

And yet, at the same time, we have a country getting older and older, meaning we need new, younger taxpayers to make sure the boomers get their social security and Medicare. (If we just turned the illegal immigrants into legal taxpayers, we'd solve the problem.) Many of our bridges and roads are crumbling before our eyes. Mental health, especially among teens, is worse than ever. And while we know how toxic the internet can be, we don't have the political will to take even basic steps that can make it safer.

And to top it all off, we live in a 24/7 world of constant information, constant contact, constant breaking news, which means we're getting pummeled relentlessly with bad stuff all the time.

Here's the final insult: our political system is completely, devastatingly broken. And because of this, there's no way right now to fix any of these problems. Occasionally one political party can muster enough votes to pass some kind of meaningful legislation, but mainly, we're stuck in one of two worlds: (a) total gridlock where everyone just fights and nothing gets done (think Congress)[1]; or (b) legislative bodies controlled completely by ideological extremes on either side who pass laws that are often patently insane (think the laws from the state of Texas that allow teachers to walk into the classroom armed or laws from the state of California requiring gender-neutral displays of toys and toothbrushes in department store windows).[2] Either way, nothing gets better.

The good news is, there is a solution to all of this. That's what this book is about. The reason I'm writing it is to persuade you that there is one way we can fix our democracy: mobile voting.

Typically, young people have organized around radical causes—civil rights, women's rights, the anti-war movement. But today, almost incredibly, the most radical possibility is finding common ground. The next great reform will come from pushing the country into the middle and forcing our government to become competent and functional again.

Virtually every American, at this point, has a smartphone in their pocket. It has become a utility, not a luxury. If we bring voting to where the people are, to where technology already is, we can exponentially increase voter turnout. Politicians make choices solely based on what it will take to win the next election. If only a small, extreme group of voters participate, their policies are extreme as a result and nothing gets done. If a larger group of voters participates, it will reflect the mainstream, which means that to keep their job, politicians need to do what most people want to see happen (cooperation, progress, and results). We can dramatically increase participation by letting people vote securely on their phones. That would change all of the inputs and all of the incentives that govern how our politicians act and what they support. And that's what leads to better policies, better laws, and a better future.

So far, through our work at the Mobile Voting Project, we've been able to test the idea of voting on your phone in seven different states (Colorado, Oregon, South Carolina, Utah, Virgina, Washington, and West Virginia), working with relatively small but key groups to prove that the concept of being able to vote on your phone can work both securely and efficiently. Mobile voting is exactly what it sounds like: opening a secure app on your phone and choosing your candidates just like you use your phone to transfer money, pay bills, talk to your doctor, arrange your love life, and everything else. (If the banks can protect our money online, we can definitely protect people's votes during the few times a year they're cast.)

People with disabilities, as well as those deployed in the military, have already voted on their phones in real elections, without any issues whatsoever. And the team at the Mobile Voting Project has taken everything we've learned from those elections and put it toward the development of new mobile voting technology that will be available, for free, to any jurisdiction that wishes to use it. We can only materially increase turnout and create a mandate for consensus, compromise, and cooperation if we make voting far more accessible— if we can meet today's potential voters where they are. Bringing all of us into the democratic process is how we change everything.

Make no mistake about it: those in power are going to use every tool they have to block us. It doesn't matter what party they belong to. There is one cause and one cause only that unites all elected officials: staying in office. Almost everybody holding an elective office right now got there by working within the existing system. What in the world would make them take a chance on a new system? Only the utter determination and passion of people like you who care enough to read a book like this.

I spent the first fifteen years of my career working directly in government and politics at the local, state, and federal levels, both in the executive branch and the legislature. I went to law school, so I have a decent grasp of how the judiciary functions. I've run political campaigns. I have seen how the system works and how the sausage is made from every angle.

But it wasn't until I started working in tech that I saw the power of mobile voting. Between 2011 and 2015, I helped run campaigns to legalize Uber and ride-sharing across the United States. I don't know how much you know or care about how the taxi industry works, but let me tell you this—before Uber arrived on the scene, this industry was as entrenched, corrupt, and as stagnant as it gets. The people who ran it liked it that way. They didn't care about customers or drivers or anybody but themselves, and the last thing they wanted was an upstart like Uber being permitted to compete with them. They had countless elected officials in their pocket and they fought us at every pass.

But we had one huge advantage, and it wasn't money or political favor. It was that when people used Uber, they really liked it. In fact, they vastly preferred it to the old taxi system. Our challenge—as Uber's political team—was how to channel this goodwill into a political force. To turn our customers into activists.

So we took the one thing they all had in common—the Uber app on their phones—and turned it into an open line to their elected officials. With the press of a button, riders could make their views count. For example, in a New York City fight where Mayor Bill de Blasio tried to effectively shut down Uber by banning any new cars or drivers, our customers were presented with the usual array of choices—UberX, Uber Black, Uber XL—but also a new option called *de Blasio*. This "de Blasio mode" informed riders that by capping the number of for-hire vehicles in the city, the proposed new law would mean a 25-minute wait time for rides and then immediately connected them to the mayor and their city council member to oppose the bill.

Both in New York City and nationwide, millions of people ultimately used the app to warn their elected officials not to take away Uber. It worked. The ease and simplicity of weighing in via the app changed the underlying politics of the issue and put Ubers on the streets of major American cities virtually overnight.

Even as one of the architects of the plan, I could hardly believe how well it worked. It was an epiphany. I remember sitting in my office thinking, *I bet all these people who are helping us win these campaigns never vote in most elections, especially most primaries. They couldn't tell you who their state senator is. They didn't vote in the primary for their representative in Congress or the city council or the county legislature.*

Why? Not because they don't care. Not because they're too lazy or apathetic to do anything. Clearly, based on the support they'd shown for Uber, they were willing to act on something when it mattered to them. It's just that the hassle of voting has eclipsed the tangible benefits, especially in primaries and races for lower offices.

Think about what voting entails. You have to get up early or skip your lunch hour to venture out to what is probably an unfamiliar location, where there might be a line or some other delay or confusion. The technology itself is typically balky and outmoded, unlike anything we use for any other activity. Voting takes you to a land forgotten by time, an experience that engenders little confidence or enthusiasm for our democracy. Given how actively we discourage people from voting, we really shouldn't complain about low turnout. It's only logical: beyond participation being logistically difficult, voters often feel like their vote won't really change anything. They feel like the election is determined solely by powerful special interests, and they feel like the system is so rigged and so corrupt that nothing can help.

What we're left with at the end of the day is a democracy dominated by the handful of registered voters who do turn out for primary elections. For example, in the 2022 congressional primaries, according to the Bipartisan Policy Center, Republican turnout was 10.6 percent. Democratic turnout was even worse at 9.3 percent.[3] This small minority of primary voters pick the nominees that the rest of us are then forced to choose between in the general elections.

And these primary voters are not a good representation of the electorate. They skew to the hard left or the hard right, they're dominated by special interests, and the candidates they pick tend to reflect those characteristics.

The Uber experience taught me that people are more than willing to engage if we give them tools that fit within the context of their lives. People manage their money on their phones. They manage their healthcare. They manage their families and their love lives. We can do pretty much anything on our phones except vote. Why?

Because the people currently in power don't want us to. Anything that threatens their hold on elected office must immediately be stopped. It's not that our politicians are uniquely bad. They're just people who desperately need affirmation and validation. That's typically who runs for office. That's just human nature. It was likely the same thing in the Roman Senate, the Greek Senate. And everything before and after.

The difference is that the way we elect people in the United States encourages the worst personality traits of our elected officials. We're cursed with a few unique causes that make U.S. politics especially bad. First, the tremendous amount of money in politics leads to endless negative campaigning (because negative ads are effective). Second, we have a winner-take-all electoral system where, unlike parliamentary democracies, there is very little room for different viewpoints or dissent from the party line. Third, our culture pioneered the notion that money or status matters more than anything else, and for most elected officials, winning office is the only way they'll ever gain power and influence, so winning office and winning at life become completely intertwined.

It doesn't have to be that way. Human nature may be immutable, at least absent millions of years for evolution, but our laws are not the Ten Commandments. They're not written in stone. They're the product of the imagination, context, intelligence, and politics of any given situation. If we want better policies, if we want better laws, if we want better outcomes, we just have to be smarter about how we go about the process, both electorally and governmentally.

I got into politics because I didn't want to lead an ordinary life. I didn't want to just get a good job as a lawyer or a banker or something, make a nice living, move to the suburbs, have 2.5 kids, and retire at sixty-five to play golf or Rummikub. I don't believe in reincarnation or an afterlife. To me, what we have right now is all we get. I wanted my existence to be more than just that of another person who comes and goes without making an impact. That felt hollow. Insufficient. And to me, when I was a young person starting out, working in government and in politics looked like the best way to have an impact.

So I did. While still in college, I worked for Ed Rendell, the mayor of Philadelphia, spending most of my days at City Hall rather than in class, because it was much more fun and because it felt useful. After college, I took a job as spokesperson at the New York City Parks Department, working for Parks Commissioner Henry Stern, who was willing to do anything for attention. From him, I learned two things—how the media works and, perhaps more importantly, how the mind of a politician works.

After that, I switched to the federal government, serving as communications director for U.S. Senator Chuck Schumer. Chuck, who later became the Senate Majority Leader, was an interesting boss because he is, in many ways, exactly what you want in a leader.

Exceptionally smart. Very hard working. Not corrupt. Generally, Chuck is not an asshole. But he's also the epitome of a politician. He wasn't about passing legislation or promoting good policies. The job was simple—get Chuck's face on TV and his name in the newspapers as often as humanly possible because his self-image and self-worth depended on it. If Chuck woke up and read his name in the paper, he felt good about himself. If his name wasn't there, he felt like a failure. So my two years working for him was nonstop press conferences, press releases, speeches, op-eds, events, hearings, publicity stunts, and anything else that made Chuck feel good. It was an outstanding learning experience.

In the wake of 9/11, Mike Bloomberg became mayor of New York City, and I got a job at City Hall creating the campaign promises initiative which made Mike the first (and still only, to my knowledge) politician ever to publicly report on the status of every single one of his campaign promises. We kept a running tally that indicated whether they were done, halfway done, or hadn't even started yet. This was a level of personal accountability that set Mike apart from every other politician I know of.

One day, while sitting in the bullpen in City Hall, I got a call from a former colleague asking if I wanted to be the deputy governor of Illinois. "What's a deputy governor, and why are you calling me?" I asked. Turns out, back then, the deputy governor ran the state. Like literally everything—operations, budget, policy, legislation, and communications. I was twenty-nine years old and suddenly had the chance to manage the (then) fifth-largest state in the country. I had to do it.

When I agreed to the job, most people still thought highly of the governor, a charismatic, handsome, enigmatic guy named Rod Blagojevich. On the retail level, at a rally or a parade or going door to door, the guy was an ace, a total natural. You couldn't *not* like him. Behind the scenes, he was a disaster, a menace to society, and that side came into full public view when he got caught trying to auction off the U.S. Senate seat made vacant when Barack Obama was elected president. Rod was sentenced to fourteen years in prison for that and two dozen other crimes and served eight years before his sentence was commuted by Donald Trump.

What made Rod interesting was that his view of politics and government was both shockingly crazy and shockingly honest. He saw his job as winning elections, not actually being governor. He would say to us, "I did my job, now you go do yours." And he meant it. Rod wouldn't come into the office for months at a time.

In the few instances where he did have to show up somewhere, we'd write a speech like the State of the State or the budget address, hand it to him a few days beforehand, and tell him to read it from the teleprompter. He didn't participate in most governmental decisions like which laws to sign and which to veto or whom to pardon or what our policy agenda should be. That job, incredibly, was left to me, then a twenty-nine-year-old New Yorker who happened to have gone to law school at the University of Chicago but otherwise had zero connection to Illinois and zero business running the state. I did the best I could with it, got some things done (universal health care for kids, universal preschool, open-road tolling, importing prescription drugs from Europe and Canada), and stayed out of trouble.

After I returned to New York, I ran Mike Bloomberg's 2009 mayoral reelection campaign. Mike is one of the few politicians

I've ever met who genuinely didn't care about politics. Of course, he
wanted to win reelection and we spent an incredible amount of his
money to help make that happen. But he wasn't willing to take a
position just to help his next election, and he wasn't willing to avoid
a controversy just because it was politically unpopular, like when he
supported the construction of a mosque near Ground Zero.

In working for both of them, I saw the exception in Mike and
the rule in Rod. But only by experiencing both was I able to start
understanding that the path to a better system is not about personalities, but about incentives. Rather than just complaining about
politicians or wishing they were somehow better people, we have to
reset their priorities. We have to make *getting things done* an absolute condition of holding office. We don't need politicians to defy
human nature. We just need them to do what already comes naturally to them—looking out for themselves.

In the case of Uber, politicians realized that while it's easier to
take a few thousand bucks in campaign contributions from the taxi
industry and do their bidding, once several thousand constituents
weighed in on the other side, the inputs shifted completely. The
way to get reelected was to not piss those constituents off. This
strategy worked especially well in the case of FanDuel.

FanDuel, an online sports betting platform, was the first investment we made out of my first venture capital fund, and early on,
it seemed like a bad choice. One afternoon in October, the *New
York Times* ran a story accusing employees of both FanDuel and
DraftKings of using insider data to bet on the other's platform and
game the system.[4] The tsunami followed—cease-and-desist letters
from multiple attorneys general and legislation to ban daily fantasy

sports betting in their states.[5] Of course the casino industry was behind this—the more people can gamble from their phones, the less reason they have to schlep to some shitty riverboat casino. But casinos are big campaign donors, and at least for Democrats, following the *New York Times*'s lead is standard operating procedure. So the incentive for the governors, state senators, state reps, and state attorneys general was clear—put FanDuel and DraftKings out of business.

It wasn't until we changed the inputs (the underlying factors that politicians use in their cost-benefit analysis to decide what's in their best political interest). The argument made so much sense. We'd mount campaigns in a state and start recruiting our customers to advocate politically both through the FanDuel app and through broad-based advertising and grassroots events. We'd hire local lobbyists and sit down with, say, a state rep in Florida.

The conversation went something like this: "You have 3,432 FanDuel and DraftKings customers in your district. Now, let's be honest. These 3,432 people? They don't vote in your primary. They don't even vote in the general election most of the time. They don't know your name. They may not even know what a state representative is. But here's what they do know: they fucking love fantasy sports betting. And if you take it away from them, then we are going to make sure every single one of them is registered to vote, knows exactly who you are, knows you're the one who took this away from them, and we are going to mobilize all of them to come out and vote against you in your next primary."

Once that sank in, the deal was done. No politician was going to risk pissing off a passionate base of constituents—even if those constituents usually are totally removed from the political process—just to make the casinos or the *New York Times* happy. Prior to our conversation, the inputs favored doing what the powerful donors and media outlets wanted. Post-conversation, the inputs were very clear—stay the fuck out of this. We ended up winning, one way or another, in every single state.

That made it clear to me that we could end much of the polarization and dysfunction that plagues our government and politics if we used the same approach for voting. After announcing the idea for the Mobile Voting Project at TechCrunch Disrupt—a giant tech conference—in 2017, we were able to put the idea to the test in 2018 in West Virginia.

Mac Warner, West Virginia's highly innovative Secretary of State, had long wanted to find a way to make it easier for members of the military deployed overseas to vote. After all, they were risking their lives to protect our right to vote and yet the system of getting ballots to foreign countries and then back in time to the election office was extremely flawed. A tech startup called Voatz produced a blockchain-based version of mobile voting, and we were able to put the parties together (with me paying for West Virginia's costs to administer the election to make it happen) to offer mobile voting to deployed military from two counties.

It worked. Turnout went up. And an independent audit from the Blockchain Trust Accelerator showed that the results were tamper proof. That validation led to mobile voting pilots in seven different states across twenty-one elections over the next few years. Depending on what each election official preferred, either a cloud-based or blockchain-based system was used to make voting by phone available to both deployed military and people with disabilities. (If you think voting is a pain, imagine being blind and dealing with voting.)

The new approach drew praise and criticism. Advocates from organizations like the National Federation of the Blind and the Drum Major Institute (run by Martin Luther King III and Arndrea Waters King) supported making voting easier and more accessible. (Leaders from both groups have essays later in this book.) Cybersecurity experts from different universities worried that the system was too easy to hack and vociferously opposed it.

To address their concerns, we decided to fund development of new mobile voting technology. There's a whole chapter in this book going into granular detail on exactly what we are building and how we're building it, but to summarize, we spent three years and $10 million to build the first and only end-to-end encrypted and end-to-end verifiable voting technology.

In 2025, we will launch that technology and make it free and open source for anyone—any jurisdiction, anywhere—to use. I believe that with VoteHub, our mobile voting technology, we have created the perfect vehicle to meaningfully increase voter turnout, especially in primaries. And that gives us the chance, finally, to change the political inputs that decide the policy outputs that impact us all, every single day.

Because until we can change the inputs, everything you worry about will probably end very badly. We won't limit the increase in warming to 1.5°C, which means we won't stop the ice caps from melting, won't stop heat waves from killing millions, won't stop the water tables from drying up, won't stop category 5 hurricanes from destroying communities, and ten other equally bad scenarios. We won't stop mass shootings in schools, Walmarts, churches, or anywhere else. We won't figure out an immigration policy that actually benefits our economy. Health care will remain way too expensive. Our schools will continue to fail to prepare students for the real world. Social media will remain unregulated and dangerously toxic. (Feel free to insert any other catastrophe that's on your mind.)

And given the continuous toxic feedback loop we've created, without fundamental reform, our problems can only get worse. Think about it. A politician is rewarded for ludicrous behavior, for saying the most vile things possible about their political enemies. The crazier the allegation (my favorite is Marjorie Taylor Green's "Jewish space lasers" claim), the more attention they get. The more likes. The more posts. The more views on YouTube or TikTok. And that's just on social media. Politicians also get to see their face all over Fox News or MSNBC and on every left- or right-wing blog that only cares about sucking you in, regardless of what's true. And to make it even worse, too many people now think that acting like an over-caffeinated imbecile is how you're supposed to behave in politics, so they mimic the behavior. Which only encourages the politicians to do it even more. And the cycle goes on and on, taking us down the drain with it.

Like any relationship, it's easy to see the country reaching the point of wanting a divorce. If you get to the point where there's no way to bridge your differences, the only solution is something new.

Would ending up as two or six or a dozen different countries be so bad? You could make a case for it. We'd share defense and infrastructure but make our own policies on everything else. You'd also be destroying the greatest experiment and greatest nation ever to grace the planet. When you don't have to.

There is only one way to fundamentally change this trajectory.

It's by changing the one truly relevant input—higher primary turnout. There's only one way to materially increase turnout and that's by making voting much easier. There's only one way to make voting much easier—by letting people vote the same way they do everything else, using the same device they take out of their pockets and stare at every thirty seconds anyway.

We should want as many people as possible to vote, especially younger people who will have to live with the choices today's politicians make for decades to come. To do this, we need to immediately dismantle the obstacles that make it hard for too many people—people with disabilities, deployed military, people on tribal lands, college students, people living through emergencies, and so many others—to exercise their basic rights.

We should make sure that voting in all forms is secure. Right now, each current form of voting—paper ballots and voting machines—has its problems. We can introduce a far more secure system of online voting that can take advantage of transformative technologies that allow end-to-end encryption, so that a ballot is protected all the way to when votes are counted, and end-to-end verification, which allows voters, election officials, and even the public to track and make sure that all votes have been collected and counted. You can't do that with a paper ballot.

And we should understand why the powers that be on both sides of the aisle desperately want to keep things the way they are, why they have no interest in making your life better at their own expense, why and how they will fight mobile voting at every turn (and all of the nonsense excuses they'll use along the way), and most important, what you can do about it.

If enough Americans stand up and demand mobile voting, if you express your support continually on Instagram, X (formerly Twitter), and Twitch, on TikTok and YouTube, to your friends and family, in newsletters and blog posts, to the people who hold elective office and those who aspire to, in meetings and rallies, in all the myriad places that politics happen, then eventually, despite the entrenched opposition, we will prevail. The same thing that can make mobile voting a reality—true democracy in action—is also the only thing that can save both our democracy and our country.

GLOSSARY

Terms that will be useful to understand when reading this book

THE BASICS OF ELECTIONS

PRIMARIES—Elections held by parties to determine who their candidate will be in the general election (the one in November). Because of gerrymandering (defined on the next page), in the vast majority of elections, only the primary matters.

GERRYMANDERING—The process that politicians use to draw legislative districts. Their goal is often to... to ensure that virtually every seat is either a safe Democratic or safe Republican district, with the vast majority of voters in that district belonging to one party ahead of the other. That means that the dominant party in each district essentially chooses the winner in the primary since whoever that person is will win solely based on their party affiliation.

ELECTORATE—Broad term referring to the total population eligible to vote in any given election. In reality, a small subset of these voters actually participate.

ELECTORAL COLLEGE—The system set up by the Founding Fathers that awards a specific number of votes in the presidential election, based on population, to whichever candidate wins that state. So if Florida has twenty-nine electoral college votes and one candidate beats the other by .02 percent, the winner takes all and everyone who voted for the other side is effectively disenfranchised. It's a huge problem.

THE ELEMENTS OF A CAMPAIGN

EARNED MEDIA—Any media that isn't paid for, so basically every newspaper, TV station, radio station, and podcast that covers politics and elections. Earned media is the most powerful tool in any campaign because the same people who run for office are the people who care desperately what is said and written about them publicly. They will do virtually anything for good press and virtually anything to avoid bad press.

PAID MEDIA—Advertising. It includes TV ads, digital ads, paid tweets and social media posts, radio and podcast ads, direct mail (oversized glossy campaign postcards), billboards, etc. Most of the spending occurs on TV ads, but with the advent and growth of streaming television, the efficacy of TV advertising continues to decline, so a major normative shift in political advertising and campaigning is coming.

DIGITAL MEDIA—A subset of paid media, ranging from pre-roll and banner ads to text and email spam from campaigns to social media ads.

SOCIAL MEDIA—What it sounds like: politicians using Instagram, Twitter, Facebook, and other platforms to spread their message and reach a wide audience without having to pay for it. It allows candidates and elected officials to bypass reporters and take their message directly to the people. However, X (formerly known as Twitter) is different from reality and many people who work in politics have a difficult time understanding this.

GRASSROOTS—Mobilizing voters to go to the polls to vote for your candidate or to express their views to politicians, usually through phone calls, emails, texts, tweets, and rallies. It allows you to leverage the passion of individuals in a way that other forms of persuasion cannot.

OPPOSITION RESEARCH—Discrediting your opponent however necessary/plausible/possible. It usually means scouring public records to find anything problematic—articles, speeches, press releases, tweets, posts, court records, judgments, liens, arrest records—and placing that information in the media. Sometimes it also means hiring a private investigator, but not that often.

POLLING—Surveying voters to find out what they think about any particular politician or issue. It's effectively a report card for elected officials—and a direct reflection of their popularity. Polling also endlessly fascinates reporters, so it is a very effective tool toward making your case.

POLICY—Can range from drafting legislation or regulations to white papers to holding conferences to writing op-eds and blog posts. Some policy work occurs on the government side either by legislative staff or executive branch staffers, but it usually takes an outside group first making the issue politically relevant enough for anyone to care about.

LOBBYING—The art and practice of directly persuading elected officials and staffers to do what you want. Lobbyists range from individual firms that take on lots of clients to trade associations for specific industries (pharma or airlines or soda companies or any other sector) to employees of companies big and small, nonprofits, think tanks, community groups, political parties, and so many others. The days where "a guy knows a guy and makes a call" are over, but individual meetings with legislators and regulators are still very important.

CHAPTER 2

....

THE TEN RULES THAT DEMYSTIFY POLITICS

Now you have the underlining definitions of most the moving parts in our political system. Over past the few years, I made a list of ten rules that explain and demystify politics as a baseline for understanding how politicians think and the factors that influence their decision-making. I find myself posting it in the chat on Zoom during speeches, classes, and meetings all the time. If you want to change things in this country, this is where the movement starts. Good ideas don't win by themselves. It doesn't matter if you're right about a given issue, even if the other side is obviously wrong. You're never going to get anywhere until you understand the nature of the game itself.

RULE 1: EVERY POLICY OUTPUT IS THE RESULT OF A POLITICAL INPUT

First and foremost, every policy output is the result of a political input. Politicians make every decision on what to support or oppose solely based on what will impact their next election. It doesn't matter that they should be better people than that. Republicans should be willing to put the safety of kids ahead of the political clout of the National Rifle Association (NRA). Democrats should be willing to put the future of kids ahead of the political clout of the teachers' unions. They're not. Sad as it is, this is reality. They put their own political needs first, every single time. Keep this in the forefront of your mind when you're listening to a speech or reading the newspaper or anything involving politics, and you'll see the world a little more clearly, I promise.

RULE 2: EVERY POLITICIAN VALUES STAYING IN OFFICE FAR MORE THAN ANYTHING ELSE

It's very hard to win your first election. You have to introduce yourself to strangers who don't care about politics and don't like politicians. You have to beg people for money day and night. You have to put yourself out there with a high degree of risk that something embarrassing about you will come out (and there's always something embarrassing). You have to tell anyone with the ability to move money or votes in your election exactly what they want to hear, regardless of what you may actually believe. It's a painful, humbling process.

But, if you're lucky enough to win, it feels so, so good. Suddenly, you are *somebody*. You get a fancy title, staff, sometimes a car and driver, a special license plate. Most people treat you differently than before. Nicer, with more respect. Lots of people representing dozens and dozens of different interests want to be your friend, give you money, and invite you to stuff. And guess what? Having people kiss your ass like this is highly addictive. Once you've both been through that first election and tasted the spoils of victory, the last thing you want is to go back to being a normal person.

Most politicians enter office determined to make life better for their constituents as a whole. They quickly learn that only primary voters and powerful special interests are taken seriously by their colleagues. No one else factors into the decision-making process on, say, which crimes should or shouldn't be eligible for bail or which books should or shouldn't be allowed in school libraries. Only the ideologues and the powerful lobbies. And no matter how well intentioned a politician is on the way in, almost all of them quickly fall in line with the same group think that puts career preservation ahead of any specific policy or idea.

RULE 3: POLITICIANS INNATELY UNDERSTAND WHAT'S IN THEIR POLITICAL INTEREST

Politicians are extremely rational and smart when it comes to determining what's in their political interest. You may think your local mayor or state senator or county executive is a moron. You may be right. But despite the inanity that comes out of their mouth on a nonstop basis, they tend to have superhuman talent for one thing—the math of their next election.

Occasionally, you can bullshit a politician about why your issue will help them win the next election or why not supporting it will cost them their next election. But these people, at least when it comes to this one issue, are very hard to fool. They know exactly who votes in their primary. They know what brings those voters to the polls. They know who those voters listen to. They know what those voters care about. You're going to have a really hard time convincing them that you know their primary voters better than they do.

RULE 4: YOU CAN'T DEFY HUMAN NATURE

Expecting politicians to do the right thing rather than the thing that benefits them politically never works. You can't defy human nature. This is why nothing ever changes after a mass shooting at a preschool. Republicans refuse to give an inch on gun control for very simple reasons. They know that in their next primary, of the 12 percent of eligible voters who will show up, half will be NRA members. They know that if they support an assault weapon ban, or even move incrementally in that direction, that will outrage the NRA and its members (we'll get into a specific, real-life example of this shortly), which means they'll be heading into their next primary with 50 percent of the electorate already pissed off at them. They never take that risk. Just to be clear, Democrats, on their own set of issues, are equally bad.

RULE 5: ONLY TWO THINGS MATTER WHEN A POLITICIAN MAKES A DECISION

Politicians will do what you want in one of two cases: (a) they think you can help them win their next election; or (b) they think you can cost them their next election. Otherwise, you don't matter at all. Their decision tree is simple: does this help me or hurt me the next time out? They're not weighing all of the different permutations and implications of different policy ideas. They're not looking at the country or their city or state or county and saying, "What's the decision that would help the greatest number of people?" They're looking at the 12 percent of voters who will show up in the next primary and do whatever they think will make them happy.

Centrist politicians who try to govern for their district or constituents as a whole are often swept out of office, especially when they decide to vote with the other party to try to get an important bill passed. A 2020 Congressional Quarterly analysis found that of the thirteen Democrats who lost their seats in the 2020 elections, eight were among the most independent voters in the House. And because most voters don't show up, those who did were typically the most partisan. They punished their representative for working with the other party and actually getting things done. This is insane.[1]

RULE 6: THE ONLY ELECTION THAT MATTERS IS THE PRIMARY

Because of gerrymandering, the only election that typically matters is the primary. And because, outside of a presidential primary, turnout is typically 10 to 20 percent, a very small group of voters and special interests choose our elected officials and the policies they pursue. You may be thinking, "Well, there's a presidential election once every four years, so that should mean that at least half of the time, primary turnout is a lot higher than 10 to 20 percent." In theory, you're right. But the politicians understand that too. And they don't want high-turnout primaries because the results are less predictable. Too many people participate. So, wherever they can, they hold presidential primaries on separate dates from the other elections to keep turnout nice and low. The politicians know who matters. And they cater solely to those voters and groups and no one else.

That's why even though Congress's overall approval rating is usually well south of 20 percent, more than 95 percent of incumbents are reelected. According to a report from the Bipartisan Policy Center, in the 2022 congressional primaries, Republican turnout was 10.6 percent. And that's considered good. It was 8.8 percent in 2018, 7.2 percent in 2014 and 9.3 percent in 2010. It's the same problem across the political aisle. In 2022 congressional primaries, Democratic turnout was 9.3 percent. That's down slightly from 9.9 percent in 2018, 6 percent in 2014 and 7.8 percent in 2010.[2] Those tiny percentages of voters are calling the shots because they show up and most people don't.

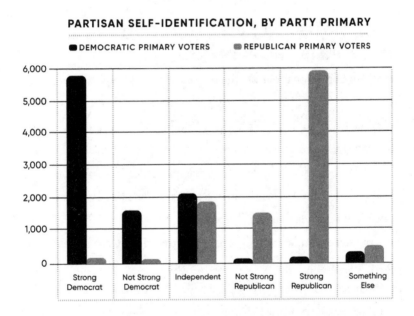

RULE 7: POLITICIANS WILL DO WHATEVER IT TAKES TO STAY IN OFFICE

Because all politicians want to do is stay in office, they will adapt to whatever policies the majority of their primary voters support. So if primary turnout expands considerably, the politician shifts to the center to accommodate it. This is good news. When you believe in nothing, you can easily shift your position to suit whatever your primary voters want.

This is a theory that can't be proven, but my bet is that if you moved 100 Democratic politicians into deep red districts and 100 Republican politicians into deep blue districts, 90 percent of them would change their position on abortion. And if they're willing to change their views on an issue as fundamental as that, imagine how quickly they'd pivot on anything else.

It's also our opportunity. If we want the two parties to feel safe working together, to not be punished in their next primary for compromising or reaching consensus, they need to believe that their primary voters want that. And at 12 percent turnout, they don't—they want purity. But what if we get to 30 percent or 40 percent? The higher turnout goes, the closer voters come to matching the population as a whole. A primary with 40 percent turnout has a far more moderate, centrist base than a primary with 10 percent turnout.[*]

Take guns. Based on most polling, around 70 percent of

---

[*] Katherine Gehl and Michael Porter's work here describes the situation well. "When members of Congress consider a bipartisan, compromise bill representing an effective solution to a major problem—unaffordable health care, a ballooning national debt, climate change—their top concern must be whether they will survive their next party primary if they vote yes. If they think that supporting the compromise bill will doom their chances—and on our biggest issues, on both sides, it almost always will—then the rational incentive to get reelected dictates that they vote no. This makes it virtually impossible for the two sides to come together to solve challenging problems. Party primaries create an 'eye of the needle' through which no problem-solving politician can pass. Therefore, our political processes fail to deliver results that benefit the public interest. There's no accountability for this failure because there's no threat of new competition." Katherine Gehl and Michael Porter, "Fixing U.S. Politics," *Harvard Business Review*, July–August 2020, https://hbr.org/2020/07/fixing-u-s-politics.

Americans agree on requiring background checks for all gun sales.[3] This is a solid base on which to formulate a reasonable gun-control policy that would improve public safety for all Americans. It demonstrates respect for human life and for the Second Amendment. But here's the problem: the 70 percent of Americans who agree on this? They don't vote in primaries. The people who do vote in primaries are the 15 percent on the left who support confiscating all guns and the 15 percent on the right who support concealed carry for everyone at all times. Winning a primary is solving for the 15 percent, not the 70 percent.

But now let's say that you can vote securely on your phone and primary turnout jumps to 35 percent. What happens then? Candidates redo the math. They move to the middle, because that's where the votes are.[*]

RULE 8: IF WE WANT DIFFERENT OUTPUTS, WE NEED DIFFERENT INPUTS

If we want different outputs, if we want different policies, we must change the inputs. The only thing that works is changing the political incentives. Everything else is just noise.

---

[*] "In fact, a Vanderbilt University poll in May 2023 found that majorities of Tennesseans from both parties support stricter gun laws for strengthening background checks and passing red flag laws to prevent gun-related violence. This included support from 80 percent of non-MAGA Republicans for background checks and 70 percent of non-MAGA Republicans for red flag laws. Unfortunately, those majorities don't vote in most primaries. So their views don't matter." Kevin Sullivan, "Nashville School Shooting Puts Focus on Tennessee Gun Laws and Safety," *Washington Post*, August 19, 2023, https://www.washingtonpost.com/politics/2023/08/19/nashville-school-shooting-tennessee-gun-laws-safety/.

RULE 9: MOBILE VOTING IS THE KEY TO CHANGING THE STRUCTURAL PROBLEMS INHERENT IN OUR SYSTEM

While mobile voting is the structural solution to the problem, the key to any campaign is to understand which politicians' support you really need and what will make them feel like you can impact their next primary. You can't win with just outrage or tweets or complaints. You win by changing the political inputs.

RULE 10: POLITICS IS MUCH LESS COMPLICATED THAN THE EXPERTS WANT YOU TO BELIEVE IT IS

Finally, this is all actually pretty simple. Politics is far less complex than people in the business—elected officials, staffers, reporters, pundits, academics, think tanks—make it out to be. The more complex it sounds, the more impressive they seem. But mostly, it's just about inputs and outputs and nothing else. It's an equation.

As we go through this book and as you go through life in general trying to make heads or tails of our political system, keep these rules in mind. Everything makes a lot more sense if you do.

CHAPTER 3

WHY PEOPLE LOST FAITH IN THE SYSTEM

n 1,000 years, assuming the human race is still around, historians may go back and determine that 1945–2020 was the best seventy-five-year period in human history. During this stretch, we saw massive gains on every meaningful metric of global well-being, from life expectancy to infant mortality to poverty to literacy rates and dozens of others. Technology exploded from radios and rudimentary TV sets to the iPhone, artificial intelligence, drones, self-driving vehicles, rockets that reach Mars, cryptocurrency, titanium bone replacement, renewable energy, and hundreds of other things that would have blown everyone's minds in 1944.

Human rights proliferated. In the United States alone, that period saw the Civil Rights Act, the Voting Rights Act, the legalization of same-sex marriage, the Clean Air Act, the right to abortion via *Roe v. Wade* (which was then taken away in 2022 in many states), the Americans with Disabilities Act, and many others.

Globally, decolonization took place across Asia and Africa. The United Nations came to life. Israel became a country. Apartheid ended in South Africa. The Paris Climate Accords were created. The United Nations created the Declaration of Rights of Indigenous Peoples. In the 1940s, 18.6 million people in Europe and Asia died from famine stemming from World War II. In 2022, 43,000 people died from famine in Somalia—still a terrible, unacceptable number, but also 99.77 percent lower than what we saw seventy years earlier.[1]

From a statistical standpoint, the world improved in almost every way imaginable from the end of World War II to the onset of the coronavirus pandemic. And yet, ironically, there is a pervasive sense that the world also *feels* worse than ever. Information is so accessible and rapidly transmissible that we see everything that happens, good and bad, as it happens. As a result, the same forces—democracy, capitalism, global liberalism, and cooperation—that produced all of these gains have also been rapidly losing popular trust.

Back in the days when people got their news from local TV, there was a simple axiom that described how producers picked their top stories—if it bleeds, it leads.[2] This is based on the theory, proven again and again, that viewers are drawn more to negative information than to positive. Bad stuff captures our attention and boosts ratings, which enables broadcasters to charge more for advertising. It quickly devolves into a race to the bottom, to the point where every night, we are treated to a litany of horrible events.

Then came the internet and a seemingly benign little provision called Section 230, tucked into the Communications Decency Act of 1996, which was passed by Congress and signed by President Clinton. Section 230, in just twenty-six words, explains why social media makes us so miserable. "No provider or user of an interactive computer service," it states, "shall be treated as the publisher or speaker of any information provided by another information content provider."[3]

Those twenty-six words were absolutely necessary to create the internet. By absolving platforms for the content posted by its users, the government enabled the fledgling industry to get off the ground. Makes sense, right? If on day one, I could post something hateful on AOL and the person I defamed could then sue AOL, the internet, as we know it, might never have flourished. The freedom needed to develop new systems, new architecture, new approaches, was essential to the birth of the internet we know today.

Over time, however, we reached a tipping point with Section 230. What was designed to protect content-neutral internet service providers began to do more harm than good, especially when the protection was extended to newly formed social media companies.

The problem is pretty simple—just like the TV stations before them, internet platforms are for-profit companies. They have a fiduciary duty to shareholders to base every decision on maximization of profits and nothing else. So, if you're Mark Zuckerberg, there are four days in your life that really, truly matter—quarterly earning calls. Every quarter, you and your top advisors hop on a call with major stock analysts and walk them through the numbers—revenue, expenses, profit, margin, and all the rest. Your share price depends on the outcome of those reports and those calls. Your net worth is largely dependent on your share price. So doing everything conceivable to ensure those calls go well is your top priority.

How does Meta make money? Mainly by selling access to you. You are the product. The more time you spend on the platform, the more they learn about you and the more they can tailor ads to your interests and passions. The more links you click, the more valuable you become. Their job is to keep you as engaged and addicted as possible.

What's the best way to do that? By feeding you negative content. Remember "If it bleeds, it leads"? Same thing holds true on the internet, only more so. Just like, sadly, the human nature of people who run for office dooms them to focus solely on reelection ahead of anything else, the human nature of everyone who uses the internet (so, everyone) is to spend more time looking at negative articles, negative posts, negative information.[4]

If you're Zuckerberg, you want to highlight and promote whatever content leads to the most engagement, the most eyeballs and the most clicks, because that's what leads to higher advertising revenue, which is what makes the people on the other end of those quarterly earning calls happy. So while you claim that all you care about is safety, that's total bullshit.[5] If that were true, teenage girls wouldn't find groups on Instagram that teach them how to cut themselves. They wouldn't have detailed guides on how to binge, purge, or engage in any other eating disorder.

And that's before we even consider the other main impact of social media, which is to force you to continually compare your actual life to the curated version of everyone else's you see on Instagram. You invariably conclude that their life is better and you feel bad about yourself. So social media is effectively the greatest unhappiness machine the world has ever produced—it automatically makes you feel terrible about yourself and everything else around you.

In fairness to all of the platforms I'm about to bash, our political leaders did a good job undermining public trust in our institutions decades before the first tweet ever posted. I'm going to give you a brief overview of how that happened. This history matters because it explains why the system today is so overloaded with cynicism, why most voters don't exercise their right to vote, and therefore why power has been concentrated in the hands of powerful special interests and those who do participate in primaries.

I was born in 1973, just as the United States was extricating itself from the war in Vietnam, which killed 65,000 American soldiers and more than ten times as many Vietnamese.[6] It certainly wasn't the first unjust war in American history, but it was the first with ubiquitous television coverage. As the war dragged on and more and more young men were drafted and shipped off halfway around the world for a cause no one really understood, public faith in the honesty and integrity of our government plunged.

Meanwhile, as this confusing, distant war was being fought, young Americans, possibly including your grandparents, were mobilizing for civil rights, major reforms that finally began to ensure equal rights for people of all races. The resistance they encountered from older generations deepened their feelings of distrust and alienation. The assassinations of Robert Kennedy and Martin Luther King Jr., within three months of each other in 1968, drove home the point even further, making the country feel like it was enmeshed in constant unrest and upheaval. Then Richard Nixon got elected president.

By the time he took the oath of office in 1969, Nixon had already been on the national political stage for years, most notably as Dwight Eisenhower's vice president and as the guy who lost to Kennedy in 1960. Like many successful politicians throughout time, gaining and holding power was Nixon's entire mission in life. When the chance to further improve his odds of reelection in 1972 popped up in the form of breaking into the Democratic National Committee's office at the Watergate complex, Nixon jumped at it. The resulting scandal, propelled by the reporting of the *Washington Post*'s Bob Woodward and Carl Bernstein, led to the nation's first and only presidential resignation. Trust in the United States government pretty much evaporated for millions of people.[7]

Things got a little better under Ronald Reagan, whose oratory skills inspired hope and enabled him to survive his own scandals, such as Iran Contra.* Bill Clinton came to office in 1992 amid a sea of scandals and lies that eventually led to the uncovering of an affair he had with an intern named Monica Lewinsky and Clinton's subsequent impeachment by the House of Representatives. He was saved by a Democratic Senate, much like how Donald Trump was twice saved by a Republican Senate.

After terrorists from the Middle East attacked the United States on 9/11, President George W. Bush spent trillions of dollars on the Iraq War, based on bogus evidence that Saddam Hussein had weapons of mass destruction that he intended to unleash on the world. As many as a million people, including thousands of American soldiers, lost their lives, while disturbing reports emerged of U.S. intelligence agents torturing and humiliating prisoners. As with Vietnam, we

---

* This was a big scandal in the 1980s that involved U.S. officials secretly selling weapons to Iran and then using the money to support a coup in Nicaragua. Iran was under sanctions so the sales were illegal, and overthrowing governments in Central America is not something the CIA should be facilitating. Jack Citrin and Donald Philip Green, "Presidential Leadership and the Resurgence of Trust in Government," *British Journal of Political Science* 16, no. 4, (October 1986): 431, http://www.jstor.org/stable/193833.

were presented with aspects of wars that we hadn't had to closely consider before. Was this what we as Americans believed in? Not everyone agreed on how to answer that question. But whatever side you were on, the government seemed lacking in credibility.

Excitement over the election of Barack Obama in 2008—the audacious hope promised by our first African American president—was blunted by the immediate quagmire of the Great Recession, which saw gross domestic product (GDP) fall by $650 billion and household net worth fall by $11.5 trillion. Though Obama could hardly be blamed for the crisis, his federal bailout of the financial institutions that engineered the mess, combined with virtually no legal consequences for any of those in charge, led to a whiplash of disillusionment and cynicism.

It was the financial crisis that sparked an anonymous person (or group of people) in Japan, writing under the pseudonym of Satoshi Nakomoto, to propose a cryptocurrency called Bitcoin as an alternative to fiat currencies run by corrupt central bankers. Meanwhile, here in the United States, a new political movement known as the Tea Party—feeding off anger over the bank bailouts and using new organizing tools suddenly available thanks to Facebook—swept the 2010 congressional elections.

The Tea Party's rapid ascent and success led to even more fractionalization. For the first time, all of the anger, all of the resentment, all of the polarization could be easily and neatly found and summarized all day, every day, on platforms like YouTube, Reddit, and Facebook (and later Twitter, Instagram, TikTok, as well as even more nefarious versions like 8Chan).[8] Out of this infested swamp crawled the greatest political villain of our time, Donald Trump.

Let me be clear about my own personal views of Donald Trump. To me, he is a truly odious and dangerous human being. But, if anything, his character flaws feed naturally into his political talent. Like every historic demagogue, he is *incredibly* talented. When he launched his campaign for the 2016 GOP presidential nomination, he compensated for his lack of funding and professional organization by resorting to tough-guy theater and killer instincts on Twitter. The television media couldn't get enough of him. What did he need with expensive ads? Trump cleverly and systematically used a combination of social media, earned media, and wildly over-the-top debate performances and public rallies to capture the attention of the Republican electorate and destroy his opponents.

Heading into the general election, Hillary Clinton had all of the conventional advantages—more money, more credentials, more institutional support, more endorsements, more staff, more expertise, more everything. She should have won easily. Everyone thought she would. What we couldn't see in the moment—but which is plainly obvious now—is that Clinton was the analog candidate, while Trump was digital. She had the old playbook. He had the new one.

The conditions that Trump took advantage of were created by Section 230, which had evolved from a necessary legal exemption that helped the internet get off the ground into a gaping breach that filled our lives with phony news, deceitful messengers and nonstop lies and distortions. In this environment, Clinton—highly qualified, but stiff and hamstrung by her husband's questionable legacy and her own history within the establishment—was utterly defenseless against Trump's surrogates. Insane conspiracy theories about pedophilia or drinking children's blood spread like wildfire.[9] Nothing was too outrageous to gain traction. Trump could tweet something vicious, racist, and categorically untrue, and it'd win him more votes every time. We know how that turned out.

And then it got much worse. In November 2020, Joe Biden won the presidential election. Though the election was close in a handful of key states, Biden clearly won. Trump then spent months trying to overturn the results of the election, even pressuring Georgia Secretary of State Brad Raffensperger to "find 11,780 votes" to give the state's sixteen Electoral College votes to the second-place candidate.[10] While election fraud has occurred from time to time in the United States over the past 250 years, most often at a local level, no one had before ever attempted to overturn the results of a legitimately conducted presidential election.

The failure to overturn the election then led to, amazingly, an armed insurrection on the Capitol, prompted and led by the then-sitting president of the United States. Protestors penetrated the Capitol, stormed the building, and sent senators, house members, and then Vice President Mike Pence running for their lives. This had never happened before in the history of our nation.

After the chaos and violence of January 6, the House promptly impeached Trump. His term was ending a few days later anyway, but removal from office would have barred Trump from ever running again.

This was the Republicans' big chance to rid the country of Trump once and for all. They blinked. The Republican-led Senate voted to let Trump off the hook.[11] This wasn't because Mitch McConnell, then the Senate majority leader, is a fan of Trump's.

They hate each other. And it wasn't because McConnell wasn't smart enough to see the opportunity to put the nail in the coffin before Trump made a comeback. McConnell sees the playing field as clearly as anyone. It's because McConnell was worried about his own primary voters back home, that tiny minority of the electorate that might just end his political career for doing the right thing about Trump. So McConnell allowed this despicable character to stay in office and have the chance to win back the White House. If that doesn't destroy your faith in the system, it's hard to see what could.

What we see in all these examples is the basic fabric of democracy being torn up again and again. We're beyond people calling each other names on Twitter. Trump's insults during the 2016 primary now seem almost quaint. When people say they don't vote because there's no point, because everything is fixed, because the people in power always hang on to power, because nothing ever gets better, it's hard to blame them.

But the result is calamitous. As more and more people lose faith in the system and fewer and fewer people vote, especially in primaries, the system becomes more and more controlled by the handful of special interests and ideologues with extreme agendas who block every attempt to reach consensus and get things done.

CHAPTER 4

WHAT WE GET FROM THE STATUS QUO

Chris Jacobs is no liberal. He spent five years as the Erie County Clerk[1] (in western New York, where Buffalo is the county's largest city). As part of his job, he processed thousands of gun permits for local residents. When he ran for Congress in 2020, he was endorsed by the National Rifle Association (NRA)[2] and won the Republican primary, largely thanks to an endorsement from Donald Trump and robocalls recorded by Donald Trump Jr. He strongly supported the construction of a wall along the U.S.–Mexico border and voted against certifying the 2020 election results declaring Biden the winner of the presidential election. All of this was completely in line with Republican politics and orthodoxy—and what you would expect a member of Congress in a conservative district to support. Then he dared to speak his mind.

On May 14, 2022, at around 2:30 p.m. at a Tops Friendly Market in Buffalo, a gunman opened fire. The gunman, eighteen-year-old Payton Gendron, was armed with a Bushmaster XM-15

AR-15-style rifle, modified to accept high-capacity magazines and multiple 30-round ammunition magazines. He also had a Savage Arms Axis XP hunting rifle and a Mossberg 500 shotgun waiting in his car. Gendron murdered ten people and injured three others.[3]

Jacobs grew up in Buffalo and served on the Buffalo school board. His real estate office is just a mile away from the site of the shooting. The shooting shook Jacobs to the core. He met with gun rights advocates and came away unimpressed by their arguments to reject new gun control measures. So, he broke with his party's long-standing position and endorsed a federal assault weapon ban, new limits on high-capacity magazines, and raising the minimum age to purchase certain weapons to twenty-one.

The reaction from his fellow Republicans was swift and merciless. Jacobs, who was running for reelection in the fall of 2022, was quickly condemned by Republican and conservative party leaders. Donald Trump Jr. accused Jacobs of "caving to the gun-grabbers."[4] Jacobs was summoned to the office of Ralph Lorigo, the chairman of the Erie County Conservative Party, and was told he no longer was their candidate. The same happened with the Erie County Republican Party. Every committee party that had endorsed Jacobs withdrew their support. Every Republican-elected official who had endorsed Jacobs withdrew their endorsement.

In other words, because he expressed support for an assault weapons ban just days after a mass shooting that killed ten people in his hometown, Chris Jacobs's political career was effectively terminated. A week later, Jacobs withdrew from the race.[5]

In an interview with NPR, Jacobs confirmed what we already

know to be the sad underlying truth of American politics today. "The issue of guns, you have to have a one-size-fits-all view on this. And if not, you're not acceptable to the Republican Party right now. I would say, you know, on the Democrats, it might be something like abortion. So I don't think that is good for either party to have that kind of view that you have to adhere 100 percent to a dogma. And I think it's one reason that things don't work here in Washington and why we're so polarized."[6]

Take a step back and think about what happened here. Ten innocent people going about their day, doing their grocery shopping, were murdered in cold blood just a mile from Jacobs's office. Ten days later, nineteen kids were shot to death in a school shooting in Uvalde, Texas. All were killed by high-powered assault weapons. The Republican Party's reaction to that horrible tragedy was the same—don't reevaluate anything, hold the line at all costs, silence all dissenters.

All Chris Jacobs did was voice support for a common-sense proposal, one that doesn't even remove the right to bear arms. And he lost his entire career just for speaking common sense, just for speaking the truth.

If we live in a society that is so polarized, so gerrymandered, and whose primaries have so little turnout and are so ideologically extreme that a member of Congress can't voice a view on an issue as clear cut as mass murder, what's the point of holding office? Why run for office if you're not allowed to say what you think, even after a mass shooting?

The implosion of Chris Jacobs's political career illuminates exactly why our politics feel so polarized and so dysfunctional. Not only can the two sides not work together; they can't even express any support for the other's point of view. The only people who can serve in office are people who don't care about any issue, any policy, any belief. They care only about staying in office and saying and doing whatever it takes to stay in office. That means people willing to adopt the party line, whatever it is (like the Republicans who refused to vote for Trump's impeachment/removal). And when staying in office means never upsetting the base, getting things done is virtually impossible.

Democrats, don't start feeling too good about yourself. You're not much better.

In the fall of 2017, Amazon announced an unusual idea. They were looking for a city to house their newest headquarters, a project estimated to cost $5 billion to build that would create over 50,000 new jobs. Rather than just having meetings and picking a city, Amazon publicly invited any city to compete for the chance to host HQ2, and 238 different North American cities submitted bids. It became a media frenzy.[7]

Cities were doing anything they could to get Amazon's attention. Boosters in Tucson, Arizona, sent a 21-foot saguaro cactus to the company's headquarters.[8] The city of Stonecrest, Georgia, offered to annex 345 acres of land, create a new city, and name it Amazon.[9] Fans at an Ottawa Senators NHL home game were encouraged to cheer for the city's bid.[10]

After several rounds of bidding, Amazon announced two winning sites in November 2018: New York City and Arlington, Virginia. New Yorkers were excited. A Quinnipiac University poll found that 57 percent of New Yorkers approved of the deal compared to just 26 percent disapproving, more than a two-to-one margin in support.[11] The city stood to gain 25,000 to 40,000 new jobs that would pay an average salary of over $150,000.[12] Add in 1,300 new construction jobs and the chance to diversify the city's economy away from its reliance on tourism and Wall Street, and it was the opportunity of a lifetime.[13]

In return, Amazon became eligible for up to $3 billion in tax incentives—incentives that were mostly available to any company that met the criteria for creating a certain number of high-paying jobs. The progressive left, however, hated the deal. They saw it as corporate welfare and a capitulation to corporate interests. Every dollar in incentives for Amazon—in their view, even incentives that were already standard operating procedure for any company—was too much. And they launched a campaign to kill the deal.

Enter Mike Gianaris, a state senator who represents the Long Island City neighborhood of Queens, which had been selected to host the new Amazon headquarters. Gianaris is known in New York politics as crafty and savvy, even for a career politician. That doesn't mean he's an expert in policy ideas. It means he really understands his voters and what they want, and he's going to give it to them at any cost.

Gianaris hadn't faced a primary opponent in a while, but he knew that the Amazon deal could spell trouble for him. Because turnout in Queens was so low, progressive groups opposed to the deal had disproportionate leverage.[14] One thing they knew how to do was get their members out to vote.

The typical state senate district in New York has around 300,000 to 350,000 residents. In the 2018 general election, Gianaris received about 72,000 votes, which is barely 20 percent of the district's total population.[15] In neighboring districts, state senate primaries averaged turnout of around 14 percent.[16] So if Gianaris did face a primary opponent, he was probably looking at turnout of around 26,572 voters, which equals about 14 percent of registered Democrats in the district.

So who are those voters? They're the Democratic equivalent of what Chris Jacobs would have faced in his GOP primary in Erie County. These are the most ideological, most left-wing voters around. They hate anyone who disagrees with them (even other Democrats). And they decide who their next state senator, state representative, city council member will be, since the district is gerrymandered and only the primary matters.

New York City could have desperately used those 25,000 to 40,000 jobs. In fact, just two years later when the global pandemic hit, the city lost over 600,000 jobs.[17] Even today, New York is still struggling to recover. The majority of people in New York City wanted Amazon to come. The majority of people *in* Gianaris's district wanted Amazon.[18] But Mike Gianaris knew that these numbers were not going to determine his personal political future. He knew that the people who would actually show up in his next primary were not like the rest of the voters in the district or the city. Gianaris knew that supporting the deal meant inviting a primary challenger and potentially losing his seat.

Gianaris did what any logical politician would do—he led the fight against the deal. Rallying special interest groups who opposed the deal for one reason or another, Gianaris did a great job sowing doubt about the project, despite its clear utility and benefit to New Yorkers. Eventually, Gianaris was able to wrangle himself a senate appointment to the Public Authorities Control Board, a little-known entity that had the legal power to block the deal. Once Gianaris was appointed to the board, Amazon saw the writing on the wall and pulled the project. Those jobs were lost to New York City forever.

A single politician chose to save a single job—his own!—over creating as many as 40,000 high-paying new ones. Stunning, really, and yet, utterly predictable. Mike Gianaris isn't stupid or evil. He's just a logical politician operating in today's system.

Now, imagine a world where turnout in Gianaris's primary was 36 percent instead of 14 percent. We're still only talking about roughly a third of voters participating, but still nearly an increase of three times over the status quo. Based on the polling of residents in that district, if 36 percent of voters were making the choice, the inputs would change with it. The broader voter base would become more moderate and mainstream, and Gianaris would shift his position accordingly.

In other words, if more people voted in state senate primaries, Amazon would have come to New York and as many as 40,000 more people there would have good jobs today. But that kind of turnout increase can't come from Rock the Vote rallies or grassroots outreach. It only happens by making voting markedly easier. By letting people vote on their phone.

Although both of these examples come from New York State, the problem isn't geographically specific. It's everywhere.

Let's take a look at Marin County, located just north of San Francisco. The Bay Area is famous for its liberalism. Progressive ideals and candidates rule the day, and cancel culture is applied immediately and viciously to anyone who strays from the left's approved talking points.

Affordable housing is an issue the far left talks about a lot. They're right—housing in some parts of this country, especially in and around San Francisco, is way too expensive. The people who do a lot of the actual work in a city like San Francisco often have to commute hours each way because they can't afford to live anywhere near their jobs. Building more affordable housing is the obvious solution.

Despite a very vocal pledge to diversity, however, residents of Marin County have found endless ways to prevent affordable housing from being built in their towns. A report from the University of California at Berkeley's Othering & Belonging Institute found that Marin County housed six of the ten most racially segregated areas in the Bay Area.[19] By requiring endless environmental reviews and community feedback, local residents are able to prevent the construction of affordable housing and the diversification of their neighborhood without ever saying, "We don't want poor people or people who look different from us to live here. We just like them in theory." Or, as the *San Francisco Chronicle* said, "While multifamily development doesn't guarantee an integrated neighborhood, the study shows that in a wealthy county like Marin, where the average home price is just under $1.3 million, strict single-family zoning all but ensures that communities will remain wealthy and white."[20]

As *The Atlantic*—not exactly a conservative media outlet—put it,

Businesses, business owners, and homeowners tend not to have the right to do what they want with their properties; instead, they have to ask city officials and their neighbors to approve their plans. This policy ensures that residents of lovely, tree-lined blocks do not get surprised by single-family homes getting razed and 19-unit buildings going up. It is also how, brick by brick, block by block, San Francisco has constructed one of the worst housing crises on Earth: Such citizen actions lead not just to the so-called preservation of neighborhood character but also sky-high rents and mortgages, worker shortages, displacement, gentrification, and climate-wrecking suburbanization.[21]

There are two ways to interpret this. The first is that San Francisco's political class is a group of self-righteous, left-wing hypocrites who say one thing but do another. If I intended this book to be an anti-woke screed, this is where I'd argue that everyone is a hypocrite. But we know that's not true. Yes, people's ideologies and actions don't always match up, but it seems unlikely that most people in San Francisco or Marin County truly want to block affordable housing, prevent racial and economic diversity, and cause more harm to the climate by making people travel further to get to and from work. The problem is that local elected bodies like the San Francisco Board of Supervisors are, here we go again, selected in *low-turnout elections*, while community boards are, by design, dominated by people who have nothing else to do but attend community board meetings, which is not a representative sample of the population. As *The Atlantic* said, "The kinds of people with the time and energy to show up at community meetings are disproportionately white, disproportionately old, and disproportionately wealthy."[22]

By deliberately making government activities—whether elections or community meetings—inaccessible to most people, we make change virtually impossible. If the people who have the time and inclination to show up on a random Tuesday to vote in a municipal primary or attend a community board meeting are only those with resources to spare, that condemns us to the status quo. People who have power like having power. That's why the people who frequent community board meetings opposing change are called NIMBYs (not in my backyard). They're not interested in making it easier for someone else to take decision-making authority from them. People who live in nice, tree-lined blocks in expensive neighborhoods love to be able to demonstrate their virtue on social media and by posting lawn signs about how progressive they are—while actually ensuring that no one poorer or darker can live among them.

It's not just the coasts either. We can see a very similar phenomenon at work in Chicago's public schools, which are notoriously terrible. The stats are beyond damning. According to *U.S. News & World Report*:

- Just 16 percent of elementary school students tested as proficient in reading. That means 84 percent struggle to read. Math is even worse. Just 12 percent of elementary school students test proficient for basic math competence. The stats are roughly the same for middle school students and even worse for high school students. In other words, three out of every four Chicago Public School (CPS) students aren't learning how to read or do basic math. [23]

- The college readiness rate is 28.9 percent. That means that even for the students who make it all the way through the process and graduate from high school, more than two-thirds of them aren't able to handle basic, rudimentary college-level work. So while they may have graduated, they probably shouldn't have. While CPS says that the high school graduation rate sits around 80 percent, the real number is 28.9 percent. (Basically, to not graduate, you have to literally never show up for school at all; if you make it through the front door, you get a diploma.) That's beyond abysmal.[24]

- Over a third of Chicago public schools are half-empty.[25] Why? Because parents are voting with their feet, pulling their kids out of public school and sending them to charter schools or leaving the city altogether. Charter schools are publicly funded but not unionized so they have greater ability to hire and retain better teachers, hold them accountable, and introduce fresh approaches to education. All of which typically leads to vastly improved outcomes. Meanwhile, as enrollment in public schools has declined by 16 percent since 2012, CPS funding from the city and state has increased by 55 percent.[26] More money is clearly not producing better outcomes.

- A study from the University of Chicago found that just 27 percent of CPS students attain any sort of college credential (two-year programs, four-year programs, certificates) within ten years of starting high school.[27] Twenty-seven percent! In Chicago, high school is a dead end for most kids.

In any normal business or in any rational setting, if 73 percent of the people involved are failing to achieve the underlying goal, you would demand radical change immediately.* Instead, thanks to the way we structure the voting process, Chicago doubled down on the status quo.

In the 2023 Chicago mayoral election, incumbent candidate Lori Lightfoot lost her reelection bid, after four tumultuous years in office, when she finished third in the Democratic primary. The two candidates who finished ahead of her and advanced to a runoff were Paul Vallas, a former head of CPS himself and vocal proponent of education reform, and Brandon Johnson, the candidate backed and funded by the Chicago Teachers Union—and who has worked directly for the CTU since 2011.[28]

This presented Chicagoans with a clear choice between a school reformer and a school status-quoer. According to Politico, "The union and its state and national affiliates have bankrolled Johnson's campaign with millions of dollars, and committed up to $2 million more through a CTU plan to apportion a chunk of monthly member dues to union PACs. A roster of labor-group members work or volunteer for Johnson's campaign to advance the union's formidable ground game."[29]

This is a clear example of a consortium of powerful special interests—interests whose views are often directly oppositional to the best interests of children in our schools—determining the next mayor of Chicago by spending incredible amounts of money on

---

* The truly sad thing is that Chicago's schools are so historically bad and the nation's public schools overall are so bad that Chicago's record was being spun as a major improvement when the actual results show it is nothing short of a disaster.

the campaign, ironically money that comes from the taxpayers in the first place. Union dues are automatically deducted from teacher salaries, and a segment of union dues are then put in a fund solely for political activity.

Turnout, all things considered, wasn't terrible in the runoff— by the pitifully low standards to which we're grown accustomed, anyway. Around 38 percent of eligible voters participated. But the composition of those voters reveals a troubling portend. Turnout among voters aged eighteen to twenty-four on the day of the election was less than 4 percent (accounting for later counted mail in ballots, that number may be slightly higher).[30]

Think about that number for a second. You're young. You live in Chicago, and hopefully you love Chicago and want to stay there forever. Maybe you're looking ahead, thinking about starting a family and about whether the school system is going to be a good place for your children. If you did, you might be alarmed to discover that less than a third of high school graduates are ready to face college and your calculus about staying in the city would change. At a minimum, you'd have to think about moving to the suburbs or, if you can afford it, consider private school options.

A core problem like chronically underperforming schools is where you'd hope that the political process would kick in and force the overhaul of the status quo. Well, it didn't happen in this case. With only 4 percent or so of these young voters making it out to the polls, Chicago voters who participated in the runoff chose the candidate who represents the status quo, the candidate who believes that the city's current education policies are working, the candidate who insists that only more money can make schools better and that any other measures of productivity are irrelevant, even after seeing funding increase by 55 percent over the last decade to little effect.

Now imagine if the roughly 96 percent of voters between the ages of eighteen and twenty-four who stayed home could have voted on their phone, just as another option, like voting early or by mail. Don't you think participation would have been a lot higher? And wouldn't it be better if the people most affected by new policy decisions actually participate in the process to decide who makes those decisions?

"Chicago municipal elections used to get a lot more turnout. This has been a very stubbornly consistent trend over the last two decades, where we see this around midthirties for citywide turnout," said Max Bever, the Chicago Board of Elections spokesperson.[31] Even the spokesperson for the Board of Elections admits the process isn't working. We can't keep going like this.

In case you're not convinced, here are a half-dozen more examples. To be clear, both the far right and far left are guilty of using low-turnout primaries to push through policies that are not something the majority of citizens want or agree with.

Abortion is America's most controversial issue

And yet, the public really isn't evenly split. According to a recent Pew study, 62 percent of Americans say abortion should be legal in all or most cases. Another 36 percent of the public says abortion should be illegal in all or most cases. So roughly two out of three Americans support the right to choose. And of the 36 percent who oppose abortion, only 8 percent of the total respondents said abortion should be illegal in all cases.[32] And yet, because of gerrymandering and low-turnout primaries, the only rational political incentive for GOP politicians in most red states is to oppose abortion in virtually all cases. That's why, since the *Dobbs* decision in which the Supreme Court overturned *Roe v. Wade* and the right to choose, we've seen Texas enact legislation banning abortion almost completely, effectively putting the views of the 8 percent above ahead of the other 92 percent (because that 8 percent votes in GOP primaries). Both state Medicaid *and* private health insurance are banned from covering abortion procedures or medication.

North Dakota banned abortion completely in all but a few exceptional situations. Again, the 8 percent imposing its will on the 92 percent. Same holds true in Alabama, Arkansas, Idaho, Kentucky, Louisiana, Mississippi, Missouri, Oklahoma, South Dakota, Tennessee, and West Virginia, as of this printing.

Think about what this all means. Collectively, the population of these thirteen states totals over 72 million people. These states are more conservative than the norm, so even if only 8 percent of people nationally believe that abortion should be illegal in all circumstances, let's be generous and say that in these states, three times as many voters feel this way. That still means 17 million people are telling 55 million people what they can and can't do with their bodies. That's not democracy.[33]

School meals

In addition to mobile voting, my foundation, Tusk Philanthropies, funds and runs campaigns around the country to make free breakfast and lunch available to kids. The idea of choosing to allow kids to go hungry is incomprehensible. It's immoral and, from every policy standpoint, incredibly stupid. In poll after poll, more than 70 percent of the public widely supports universal school meals.[34] We conducted a poll in North Carolina, where their legislature is Republican-controlled, that showed that over 70 percent of *Republicans* support school meals. In addition, 71 percent of Evangelical Christians, a key voting block for the GOP, support universal school meals, even after they receive conservatives' messages on cost and personal responsibility. Unlike abortion, school meals are not controversial. At all.

If you were starting a country from scratch and made a list of your very highest priorities, would anything come above feeding children?

And yet, among congressional Republicans, there is clear opposition to funding school meals. In June 2023, the Republican Study Committee released its desired 2024 budget. In it, one of their top priorities is eliminating the community eligibility provision, or CEP, from the School Lunch Program. Why? Because "CEP allows certain schools to provide free school lunches regardless of the individual eligibility of each student."[35] Three-quarters of House Republicans belong to the Study Committee, so this is not the position of a few crazies. And odds are, if you put each member of the Study Committee on truth serum, the vast majority would probably admit that feeding kids in schools is a good idea. But, supporting school meals—let alone expanding them—does not appeal to the 10.6 percent of Republican voters who typically vote in House primaries.[36] And so if you're a typical House Republican, you're forced to choose between reelection and letting kids go hungry. Not surprisingly, they're letting kids starve.

Banning books from libraries[*]

A 2022 poll sponsored by the American Library Association found that 70 percent of voters opposed banning books from public libraries.[37] Nearly three-quarters of public school parents expressed a high degree of confidence in school librarians to make good choices about which books to offer students. And this is not divided along partisan lines. Among Republican respondents, 70 percent opposed banning books from libraries, 87 percent said libraries play an important role in their communities, and 70 percent said they have confidence in local librarians to make good decisions. Opposition to banning books was even higher among Democrats. But even if we just limit consideration to Republicans, seven out of ten don't want politicians deciding which books their kids can and can't read. And yet, statistically, those seven out of ten typically don't vote in state senate primaries. At least statistically, they don't vote in state representative primaries. They don't vote in city council primaries. Most of them don't even vote in House, mayoral, or gubernatorial primaries. Of course, some of them do vote in these elections. But the tiny turnout numbers in primaries means, mathematically, that the vast majority of them do not. Which means they effectively don't matter.

You know who supports banning books from libraries? A high percentage of Republican primary voters—not Republicans overall, but the small percentage of Republicans who actually vote in primaries.[38] A study from PEN America, the nation's leading

---

[*]   I'm admittedly not objective on this issue. I love books. I own a bookstore in Manhattan called P&T Knitwear. I cofounded the Gotham Book Prize. I read constantly. The book you're reading right now is my third book, and I'm hoping to write a lot more. But with that said, this is not an evenly divided issue by any means.

organization dedicated to authors' freedom of speech, found that nearly 1,500 different books were banned from school libraries in the first half of the 2022–2023 school year alone.[39]

Book bans are most prevalent, not surprisingly, in Florida, Missouri, South Carolina, Texas, and Utah, all states that are almost exclusively controlled by Republican legislatures and governors. State legislation doesn't ban specific books but it creates prohibitions on providing student with, for example, sexually explicit material, which then allows school boards and local activists to successfully demand the removal of specific books.[40] Now, most Republicans in those states *do not want* books banned. They do not want politicians to replace librarians. They do not want politicians deciding which books their kids are allowed to read. But they don't vote in local primaries in numbers high enough to override the vocal minority. So their view doesn't matter. A small group making decisions for everyone else—something the far right, in many other circumstances, would refer to as "tyranny."[†] The problem isn't any better across the aisle.

Defund the police

Here is a direct quote from the Democratic Socialists of America (DSA) platform: "Defund the police by rejecting any expansion to

---

[†]   A newer version of this is occurring in West Virginia where, as Leif Weatherby, director of the Digital Theory Lab at New York University, says, "The state…is engaging in a kind of educational gerrymandering." Significant portions of West Virginia University's humanities and liberal arts program were cut. "The humanities are under threat more broadly across the nation because of the perceived left-wing ideology of the liberal arts." Leif Weatherby, "Opinion Guest Essay: What Just Happened at West Virginia University Should Worry All of Us," *New York Times,* August 20, 2023, https://www.nytimes.com/2023/08/20/opinion/west-virginia -university-cuts.html.

police budgets or scope of enforcement while cutting budgets annually toward zero."[41] Toward zero. In other words, a lawless society. No
police. No law enforcement. No prison. No punishments for rape or
murder or assault. Just total chaos. If these were just more words in
a manifesto from some crank organization that no one ever listens
to, that'd be one thing. But it's not. Here are some of our elected
officials who have vocally endorsed the DSA position on defunding the police: members of Congress including Alexandria Ocasio-
Cortez, Jaamal Bowman, Ilan Omar, Cori Bush, and Rashida Talib.
Among others are Chicago Mayor Brandon Johnson, New York
City Comptroller Brad Lander, and Philadelphia District Attorney
Larry Krassner. The list goes on.

But while the position was popular among DSA supporters
and high-turnout Democratic primary voters, it is not the view of
most voters or even most Democrats. A 2020 YouGov poll found
that just 16 percent of Democrats and 15 percent of Republicans
supported cutting funding for the police.[42]

Let's repeat that—84 percent of Democrats and 85 percent
of Republicans opposed *any* funding cuts for police, let alone
"cutting budgets annually toward zero" as the DSA suggests. Not
only has the vocal minority of defund supporters managed to
help pass legislation in multiple states banning bail that have led
to increases in crime, but their embrace of defunding the police
has also helped lead to the defeat of Democratic candidates in
elections across the country. That's why President Biden has
aggressively distanced himself from the defund movement. And
yet the politicians supporting the movement know exactly what
they're doing. Turnout in their primaries is typically very low and

those voters are the outliers who support defunding the police. So when forced to choose between their own political best interest and keeping people safe, the politicians choose themselves. Shocking.

Renaming San Francisco's schools

In January 2021, the San Francisco school board announced that forty-four schools—more than a third of the city's total—would be renamed because the original namesake was a colonizer, exploiter of workers, or oppressor in some other way. Now, stripping public schools and parks of names honoring Confederate generals is one thing. But among those who San Francisco banned were: Abraham Lincoln, George Washington, Thomas Jefferson, Theodore Roosevelt, John Muir, Paul Revere, and Dianne Feinstein.[43]

Abraham Lincoln. The guy who issued the Emancipation Proclamation and waged the Civil War. Dianne Feinstein who was a leader of California Democrats for decades. John Muir, known as the father of our National Park System. Paul Revere? You mean the guy who helped win the Revolutionary War? I think George Washington may have had something to do with winning the war too. Put aside that the school board failed to do even cursory research to form most of its decisions. The fact that members of the board are elected tells you everything you need to know about the pitfalls of low-turnout primaries.

In this case, the proposal was so absurd, so beyond the pale, that even San Francisco residents vigorously expressed their disapproval—to the point where the board had to take another vote that April. All six members agreed to ignore their previous edict and leave things as they were. That's an example of democracy eventually working, but only after things had first gone wildly wrong.

Safe spaces on campus

I teach a class at Columbia Business School called the Economics and Politics of Digital Disruption. The course distills lessons from my day job as a venture capitalist where my fund invests in early-stage tech startups in highly regulated industries and then handles the regulatory and political efforts necessary to allow disruption to occur (companies from our portfolio like Lemonade, FanDuel, Ro, Bird, Coinbase, Circle, Alma, Wheel, Sunday, and so on). Over the semester, students are assigned a fictitious startup around a new technology (such as flying cars, delivery drones, self-driving trucks, and crypto mining) and they develop a campaign plan to legalize their product in specific jurisdictions. Experts in lobbying, earned media, social media, paid media, opposition research, polling, and grassroots efforts speak to the students about what they do and how government works. Among the things I try to help my students understand is that successful venture capitalists can't invest in companies that only have a blue-state or red-state business model. We need our portfolio companies to operate everywhere and sell to everyone. Which sometimes means dealing with people we strongly disagree with.

Columbia, which is in New York City, is a very left-leaning campus. That much I knew going in. But I figured the business school was probably a little different. So when I had several top Republican lobbyists and staffers come in to speak to the class,

I wasn't expecting a hostile reaction from my students toward our speakers or that I would receive complaints from those who said they had been triggered by the speakers. But that's what happened.

So the next semester, before I brought some of these speakers back into my classroom, I spoke extensively to the students beforehand about being respectful and the need to learn how to at least understand and deal with people you disagree with. And then I did it again the following year. The students, after much lecturing beforehand by me, handled the speakers better. Some still complained to my teaching assistant afterward. But others came to me and thanked me for being willing to force the issue, a risk most of the career academics at the school could never afford to take.

Shielding students from material knowledge they need to do their jobs properly isn't progressive. It isn't respectful. It's dangerous—just as dangerous as Republican efforts to ban books. And my experience was extremely mild compared to what is happening on campuses around the country.

University presidents are obviously not elected by regular voters. They're typically chosen by the school's board of trustees, who solicit feedback from the faculty, staff, alumni, and many others. Once you're in office as president, the best way to lose power before your term concludes (or the best way to not get your contract renewed) is to generate significant controversy and opposition from the students and faculty. So like any politician making a decision solely based on reelection, university presidents seek to avoid any activities that threaten their ability to stay in power. That means not upsetting the people with the loudest voices. So they give in to crazy demands for safe spaces that deny free speech, prevent students from hearing diverse views, prevent diverse speakers from teaching and lecturing, prevent students from learning how to function in the real world, and generally undermine the entire purpose of a university.

It's exactly like the Republican politician who puts his reelection ahead of the kid who needs a free lunch or the Democrat who puts her reelection ahead of making local public schools better. University presidents respond to perverse incentive structures with the same inherently selfish decisions. As do union leaders, heads of many foundations, and presidents of cultural institutions.
When small groups of constituents can dictate someone's chances of gaining and staying in power, we all suffer the consequences of their narrowly but deeply held beliefs. And it keeps happening—in politics, in higher education, in labor unions, and so many other areas. Again and again.

Why? Because we let it happen. It doesn't have to be this way. We don't have to empower the voices of a few on either side ahead of the views and needs of the many. But to take power back, we have to change the system—structurally, electorally, fundamentally. That means supporting ideas like mobile voting.

PART 2

WHY VOTING IS HARD

And How People Have Tried to Make It Better

CHAPTER 5

....

WHY VOTING IS UNNECESSARILY DIFFICULT FOR FAR TOO MANY

For many of us, the barrier to voting is simply that the process is too inconvenient. Sure, we care about our government, but we're also pretty busy. And as we saw in the previous chapters, trust in American government continues to dwindle as the problems of our day and age seem to get worse. But regardless of whether we choose to use our right to vote, some groups face far greater challenges to exercising that right than others. That needs to change.

MILITARY AND OVERSEAS VOTERS

Let's start with military and overseas voters. Absentee voting started when soldiers fighting in the Civil War were among the first granted access to vote by mail ahead of the 1864 presidential election between Abraham Lincoln and former general George McClellan. (Lincoln won easily.) It makes sense, right? People putting their lives at risk to defend their country ought not to be deprived of their right to vote. During World War II, Congress tried to enfranchise soldiers deployed overseas through legislation that guaranteed access to a universal federal ballot by mail.

Today, nearly four million active-duty military, their families, and other citizens residing outside the country are eligible to vote by absentee ballot under the Uniformed and Overseas Citizens Absentee Voting Act of 1986 (UOCAVA).[1] However, a well-intentioned law like UOCAVA doesn't fix all of the logistical challenges of making sure that every American in every far-flung corner of the world gets a physical ballot in time to decide, vote, mail it back in, and have it counted in the actual tabulation. It's just too complicated to conduct via the postal system.

Because of the concern about delays in sending and receiving paper mail and the security of foreign postal systems, a majority of states already give military and overseas voters the option to return ballots electronically. Most electronic ballot-return methods involve sending the voted ballot and accompanying affidavit form by fax, by email as PDF attachments, or by uploading the PDFs to an online portal or file transfer site. With the level of technology now available, this process is like using a horse and buggy when you've got a Corvette sitting in the garage.

Existing electronic ballot-return options do not adequately meet the needs of UOCAVA voters. The typical UOCAVA voter needs access not only to a computer or mobile device, but also to a printer and possibly a scanner in order to print and sign their ballot affidavit and then, in some cases, a fax machine to upload it for electronic return. (In the private sector, I haven't seen a fax machine in anyone's office in at least two decades.) Each of these ballot-return methods also requires the voter to give up their right to a secret ballot, because there is no way election officials can separate their identity from their marked ballot.

Each of these ballot-return methods also carries tremendous security risks, giving voters no ability to verify whether the ballot received by the election office is the same as the ballot they cast. Email return options are even riskier for election officials. Election officials must open email attachments from unknown email accounts, a practice that is routinely cited as a cybersecurity risk that could threaten other parts of the election system, including voter registration databases.

These deficiencies explain why military and overseas voters continue to vote at some of the lowest rates. Domestic voters were ten times more likely to vote in 2020 than overseas voters, and while some overseas voters may take less interest in politics back home than those of us who live here, most of them plan to come back at some point so the disparity in turnout cannot be explained solely by voters having a different focus.[2] Participation in primaries and local elections is even far, far lower.*

VOTERS WITH DISABILITIES

But the problem is not limited to people abroad. One of the most important civil rights laws passed in our nation's history, the Americans with Disabilities Act (ADA), guarantees that the 61

---

* UOCAVA turnout data is not typically reported in non-general elections, and the Federal Voting Assistance Program reports biennially on participation in federal general elections only. But anecdotal data, for example data reported from the city and county of Denver, shows significantly lower turnout among UOCAVA voters in local elections in 2011, 2015, and 2019.

million Americans with disabilities have equal access to public facilities, including voting.[3] Data from the 2020 Census indicates that there are 38.3 million eligible voters with a disability, representing a nearly 20 percent increase since 2008 and comprising nearly 23 percent of the overall voting population.[4] That means voters with disabilities now make up a larger share of the electorate than Black (29.9 million) and Hispanic (31.3 million) voters.[5] And since nearly all of us will experience temporary or permanent disability at some point in our lives, the ADA has the potential to affect almost all of us.

Despite the federal guarantee to equal facilities in the ADA, voters with disabilities continue to face strong barriers to voting. Voters with disabilities were twice as likely to report difficulties voting as voters without disabilities, and 17 percent were unable to vote independently without difficulty, including voters casting a ballot in person and by mail.[6] Blind people face particular barriers to voting, with more than 22 percent reporting difficulty voting by mail and just 54 percent reporting they were able to successfully vote in person without problems.[7]

Think about it. You're blind. Your day-to-day life has plenty of challenges already. If you want to exercise your basic right to vote, you not only have to get to a polling place, but then you have to find someone there to help you. Anyone who has voted regularly knows that while sometimes things go just fine at the polling place, oftentimes they don't. And that's for people with sight. In a world where smartphone technology has made life so much easier for the blind, for the deaf, for so many people with disabilities, denying them the ability to use that same technology so they can vote like everyone else is just cruel. (And that's before we even get into absentee ballots, which are not accessible for any voter who is blind or has a print disability, which forces those voters to lose the secrecy of their vote and rely on someone else to fill out and return their ballot.)

Consider the experience of Ruth Sager, a blind voter in Maryland.[8] She filed suit in federal court following her experience of voting in person in 2018. When she arrived to vote that year, the single accessible voting machine at her polling location was not working, and the poll workers' only solution was to offer her two election judges to read her paper ballot to her and mark it on her behalf. This solution was a total violation of her privacy. Unfortunately, Ms. Sager's experience is not unique. In fact, she reported that in her twenty-five years voting at the same polling place, she remembered only two times when the accessible voting unit was set up properly.

Survey data from the National Federation of the Blind from 2020 shows the situation may be getting even worse. In its survey report on the 2020 election, the NFB found that fewer blind voters reported that accessible voting equipment was set up at polling locations in 2020 than in prior years. Just 54 percent of blind voters reported being able to cast their vote without problems, a decline from as high as 87 percent in 2008.[9]

These barriers have created a segregated and unequal voting process for people with disabilities. The result is depressed turnout and significant voting gaps among this population, as illustrated in the chart on the next page, covering the 2016 and 2020 presidential elections.

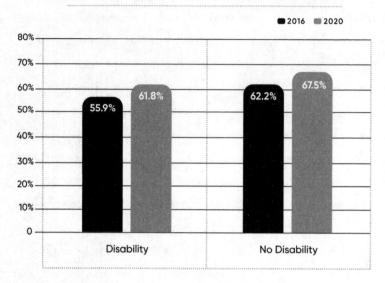

DISABILITY AND VOTER TURNOUT IN 2016 & 2020

Turnout in 2016 by voters with disabilities was 55.9 percent nationally compared to 62 percent among voters without disabilities, a six-point gap that expands to nearly eight points when adjusted for race, age, and other demographic data.[10]

In 2020, when most states expanded access to vote by mail, the turnout gap for voters with disabilities fell to 3.6 percent, affirming that when transportation and physical location barriers are removed, more voters with disabilities are able to vote.* In spite of those efforts though, voters with disabilities are still twice as likely to face difficulties voting as voters without disabilities.[11] This is not acceptable.

---

* Note: When adjusted for age, the turnout gap in 2020 was over 7 percent, according to the Election Assistance Commission.

VOTERS IN CLIMATE EMERGENCIES

In a world where climate disasters continue to displace more and more people, what about voters experiencing emergencies during an election? The pandemic exposed the need for more resilient voting options to ensure all voters can exercise their right to vote, even in emergencies.

In 2020, voting by mail was the go-to option to ensure voters could vote for president, governor, senator, congressmembers, and representatives in local, county, and state legislatures without forcing them to risk their health. And it worked. Turnout was the highest in a century, and evidence shows that the increase in turnout was highest in states that conducted the election entirely or mostly by mail. (To be clear, while I think mobile voting is the best way to empower younger voters and more voters in general, vote by mail is a wonderful reform and the two are complementary, not mutually exclusive.)

Voting by mail has been a step in the right direction to make voting more resilient. But it doesn't work in all emergencies. In 2020, COVID-19 was the biggest threat to voting across the country, but it wasn't the only one. In western states, wildfires displaced tens of thousands of voters in the weeks ahead of the election, especially in California, Colorado, and Oregon.[12] Voters were forced to flee their homes, along with first responders deployed to assist in emergencies, limiting their access to mail and making voting by mail cumbersome at best and impossible at worst. Similarly, in 2022, category 4 Hurricane Ian devastated densely populated counties in Florida, displacing thousands of voters ahead of the midterm elections and forcing state and local election officials to consolidate and relocate in-person polling sites. The Florida governor had to issue an executive order to enable absentee ballots to be sent by forwardable mail.

Hurricane Ian was certainly not the first storm to affect Florida voters in a general election. Just four years earlier, Hurricane Michael, a category 5 storm, tore through multiple counties in Florida's Panhandle, forcing state and local officials to similarly scramble to identify ways to help affected voters get a ballot. Despite their best efforts, turnout in the affected counties was depressed by at least 7 percent compared to the state turnout average.[13] Given that the race for governor that year was within 33,000 votes, the inability to vote electronically may have changed the outcome.[14]

All evidence points to worsening hurricanes and more devastating wildfires in the years to come. On average, 1.2 million Americans are displaced every year due to natural disasters, while thousands of first responders are also called to duty outside their home jurisdiction.[15] On top of that, about 600,000 patients are hospitalized every day—and that's without a global health pandemic where the next one could involve transmission by touching something, which then makes voting by mail unusable. The world is only getting hotter and the climate is only getting more and more disrupted. Voters in emergency settings are only going to become more commonplace. We need to be ready for that.

NATIVE AMERICAN VOTERS

Now let's consider tribal communities. Native Americans have long struggled for full citizenship rights. Despite the Fourteenth

Amendment's enactment in 1868 and subsequent federal laws in the early twentieth century granting Native Americans citizenship, the voting rights of most Native American voters were not fully protected until passage of the Voting Rights Act in 1965.[16]

Nearly sixty years later, many voters in tribal communities still face serious barriers to the ballot box. In fact, the Native American Rights Fund noted in a recent report that "every barrier imaginable is deployed against Native American voters."[17] Many voters in tribal communities struggle even to register to vote since they often have no standard address needed to determine their voting precinct. In-person voting is typically inaccessible, as tribal community voters may live as many as 150 miles from the nearest polling place. The Native American Voting Rights Coalition found that 32 percent of respondents in South Dakota said the distance from polling places affected their decision about whether to vote, and census data shows that over 13 percent of Native American households lack access to a vehicle.[18] Voting by mail is also difficult, because at least 18 percent do not have home mail delivery.

These obstacles help account for the fact that Native Americans have the lowest voter turnout rate of any racial or ethnic minority group in the United States. According to data from the National Congress of American Indians, only two-thirds of eligible Native Americans are registered to vote, compared to 73 percent of all eligible citizens, and voter turnout averages between five and fourteen points, lower than other minority groups.[19] Our history with Native Americans is beyond shameful already. Can't we at least make it easier for tribal communities to vote?

NONWHITE VOTERS

Like Native American, other groups of voters have also long been excluded from the voting process and consequently vote at lower rates than white voters. After the Supreme Court's *Shelby County v. Holder* decision in 2013, which weakened the Voting Rights Act by striking protections for minority voters in states with a history of racial discrimination, many of the protections in the Voting Rights Act were effectively dismantled. According to the Brennan Center for Justice, twenty-five states passed laws that have imposed new restrictions on voting in the years following *Shelby County*, such as strict photo ID laws, cutbacks in early voting and vote by mail, and registration restrictions.[20]

Many of these measures have made it harder for nonwhite voters to vote. In a 2020 poll about voting experiences, the political website FiveThirtyEight found that 24 percent of Black respondents reported waiting in line for over an hour at polling places, and Hispanic respondents were more likely to report difficulties getting off work or trouble accessing a polling place.[21] Black voters are also more likely to have trouble voting by mail. An audit in Washington State in 2020 found that Black voters' mail ballots were rejected at four times the rate of white voters' ballots. The audit found that other nonwhite voters were more likely to have rejected ballots.[22] Other states have similarly reported racial disparities in absentee ballot rejections, including Florida and Georgia. In Texas, wide racial disparities were found in absentee ballot rejections in the 2022 primary election, including evidence that nonwhite voters were 30 percent more likely to have an absentee application or ballot rejected.[23]

What does that lead to? Depressed turnout among nonwhite voters. In 2016 and 2020, the turnout gap between white and nonwhite voters was over 12 percent, up from 8 percent in 2012.[24] These difficulties demonstrate that systemic issues continue to inhibit all eligible voters from accessing the ballot box.

In March 2023, I moderated a panel at South by Southwest (SXSW) about mobile voting and civil rights.[25] The panelists, in my view, got it exactly right. Here's what they had to say:

Martin Luther King III: *"Until people are engaged, my dad and mom showed us throughout the modern Civil Rights Movement that it only takes a few good women and men to be engaged and we need to stay engaged or we might lose our democracy... Dad used to say that a voteless people is a powerless people, and one of the most important steps we can take is that short step to the ballot box. The major goal ought to be to get everybody in our country participating. That makes our democracy better. Not 67 percent and thinking, 'Oh that's great; 67 percent of the voters voted.' ... Why are we who are supposed to be the leaders not doing that?"*

Civil rights leader Ralph Neas: *"Getting involved in civic engagement, getting involved in political campaigns, getting involved in a way that you think will make a difference. There is so much out there... Change is going to happen at the local level. We've got to build movements if we're going to change Congress, and you can have a tangible result if you get involved in a meaningful way and organize and* *try to make people understand things can change. Ranked-choice voting and mobile voting, I think, are the two most important new changes. You're smart to do it on the local and national level, and I hope there's going to be ballot initiatives on this—things we can win on and build confidence and build organizations and convert it into things that will change Congress, that will change the national laws."*

Michigan Secretary of State Jocelyn Benson: *"The reason why democracy thrives is when people stand up and demand that it does. You can't expect those who have gained power through one mechanism to necessarily support policies to change how power is granted in our country or in our states. It's historically only been when people stand and demand a democracy that ensures every voice is heard and every vote is counted that we actually see the changes that open up and create a more inclusive democracy, which in this moment is now more critical than ever as our country becomes increasingly diverse. We have an opportunity to really, truly become a multiracial, multi-ethnic democracy with shared and expanded power, inclusive power, all across our country. Standing in the way of that are politicians who don't want to lose the traditional ways in which they've sought power and open it up to a more inclusive democracy."*

Drum Major Institute President Arndrea Waters King: *"Whenever there is any type of new innovation or new idea, it is certainly most readily met with skepticism* *and restriction. I think that having young people use mobile voting—this issue is something that's extraordinarily important, particularly to the young vote because they're on college campuses—not all young people are in college but they certainly are able to vote mobile-y because you're in between physical addresses. I think we also have to realize that this generation is growing up with the intuitive knowledge and comfort with being to operate mobile-y, and so for them, it makes sense that [mobile voting is] talking their language and interfacing in a language they can understand... If you don't think that your right to vote is powerful, then why are they trying so hard to take that right away from you?"*

I want to repeat Arndrea's last line because it's so accurate and powerful: If you don't think that your right to vote is powerful, then why are they trying so hard to take that right away from you?

YOUNG VOTERS

And then there are younger voters. In the more than fifty years since the Twenty-Sixth Amendment lowered the voting age to eighteen, voter turnout among young people has remained frustratingly low. A lot of them would like to vote. They care about society. They care about our government. They care about politics. If you're reading this book, I know this includes you. But the way we vote doesn't fit with the way you live.[*]

---

[*] Studies on voting barriers for young voters include research published by Sunshine Hillygus, political science professor at Duke University, and by Tufts University.

Young voters are more likely to be transient at the time they come of age to begin voting, meaning they need to register to vote or update their voter registration far more frequently than their older counterparts.[26] Any barriers to voter registration—including a lack of online registration, on-campus registration services, automatic registration, and same-day registration—mean that many young voters are excluded from the election process altogether.

Young voters also have difficulties accessing in-person options due to scheduling or transportation barriers. They are more likely to have inflexible schedules, attending college or working hourly positions, and are less likely to be able to access in-person voting options during open polling hours or to wait in hours-long lines.[27] Young voters are also less likely to own a car, and accessing other transportation, such as rideshare and public transit, can be expensive and time-consuming.[28] Confusing rules about absentee ballots coupled with postal delivery delays also make voting by mail more difficult for younger voters.[*]

All of these obstacles combine to make voting difficult for younger voters, which is why the turnout gap for voters under twenty-five remains high. In 2020, for example, the turnout gap for young voters under age twenty-five was 16 percent compared to voters twenty-five and older, according to census data. Voters under twenty-five were half as likely to vote in 2020 as voters over

---

[*]   A July 2020 poll found that half of voters under thirty-five did not have enough information to vote by mail, according to NPR. (Juana Summers, "Poll: More Than Half of Young People Lack Resources to Vote by Mail," NPR Morning Edition, July 30, 2020, https://www.npr .org/2020/07/30/896993401/poll-more-than-half-of-young-people-lack-resources-to-vote -by-mail). For example, George Washington University students were unable to vote in the 2022 midterms due to ballot delivery delays and mailbox issues.

age sixty-five. The numbers were far worse in 2016, when the gap was over 20 percent compared to voters twenty-five and older, and grew to over 30 percent compared to voters over sixty-five.[29] Other research shows that young voters are much less likely to vote in primaries, which is where relatively small constituencies yield disproportionate power.[30] And in local elections, young voters are fifteen times less likely to vote.[31]

Imagine you run a company that is promoting a new product—let's call it a new VR headset. All of the growth for the headset, its entire future, rests in the hands of younger customers. If they embrace the product, the future is bright. If they ignore it, there's trouble ahead. Now imagine that you decide to only make the headset available on the QVC shopping network and through mail-order catalogs. How many young people do you think ever look at those things? How many will go to the effort of mailing something in to order the headset? Very, very few. Democracy is the same way, except a lot more important.

CHAPTER 6

....

HOW REFORMERS ARE WORKING TO MAKE VOTING EASIER

You may be thinking, "Okay, I get it. The voting process is messed up. Mobile voting sounds like an interesting solution. But I've heard about a lot of different types of election reforms, not just this. So how do they all fit together?" Good question.

There are a number of very good reform ideas out there propelled by passionate, smart people who want to save our democracy and our country. Here's a quick primer on other key reforms and why they matter, but also how mobile voting is different.

ANTI-GERRYMANDERING

If we could make just one change to our electoral system, ending gerrymandering would be the first target. Gerrymandering, as a reminder, refers to the way legislatures draw their districts for personal benefit. Rather than using a predefined standard, they're typically free to literally construct each district block by block to ensure that the Democrat or Republican (depending on which type of district it is) will win the general election. By fixing the outcome to suit one party or the other, gerrymandering undermines the entire point of free and fair elections.

Ending gerrymandering would solve a lot of problems. Right now, legislative districts for every office from city council to Congress are drawn by whoever is in power in each state. As of now, only four states have truly independent commissions (Arizona, California, Colorado, and Michigan—five if you count Maine's split control), and some states pretend to have independent commissions. (Hawaii, Idaho, Montana, New Jersey, and Washington have political commissions run by politicians and partisan appointees.) But most states plainly use their current power to ensure their future power.[1]

As crazy as this sounds, here's how it works in most places: every ten years, the census comes out. Based on the census results, new legislative districts have to be drawn to ensure they're all still of relatively equal population size. This gives the party in charge at that particular moment the ability to decide where the lines for legislative districts get drawn. Both parties, when in power, do the exact same thing: they create districts that are overwhelmingly Democratic or Republican so that whoever wins the primary pretty much automatically wins the general election. In states where there is an independent election commission, you often see both parties still doing the same thing— strongly arguing for and using political pressure on behalf of highly partisan districts on both sides that favor incumbents.

This all but guarantees that the same politicians—the same city council members, the same state representatives, the same state senators, the same members of Congress—get reelected time and time again. Because once a candidate makes it through the primary, it's just about impossible to lose the general election when the vast majority of residents in your district are also members of your party.

So what does that mean? Exactly what we've been discussing this whole time. All you need to do is make the sliver of voters who turn out for primaries happy and you're golden. Typically, those voters are the most partisan, the most ideological, and the least interested in finding consensus or compromising or working with the other party. And because primary turnout is so low, special interests from oil companies to teachers unions have a disproportionate amount of power because just threatening to spend real money working against whichever politician dares defy them is usually enough to keep everyone in line.

The higher we can push voter turnout, the more we dilute the power of any one special interest group. But in a low-turnout election where a few hundred or a few thousand votes make all the difference, the threat of the auto dealers or construction unions dropping real money and resources into your next primary is terrifying.

There have been significant efforts to curb gerrymandering and even outlaw it altogether, though of course, low turnout is a barrier to passing electoral reforms just like it's a barrier to electing politicians incentivized to work together.[2] Well-meaning reformers have argued that districts should be drawn by independent experts who have no partisan affiliation or stake in the outcome of any specific election. There are at least a dozen different proposals out there on how to create districts that are fairer and more competitive. Occasionally, a state legislature goes so above and beyond the boundaries of fairness that the maps they draw are struck down by the courts, especially if the maps are not compliant with the Voting Rights Act. But the limitations placed on gerrymandering are very narrow and mainly ineffective. To make matters worse, the Supreme Court has made it clear that they will not outlaw gerrymandering or tell states how to manage it differently.

Why wouldn't the Court want to make things better? Because their appointments are political too—the president nominates them. So while federal judges, once confirmed, have lifetime tenure, many remain strongly loyal to the best interests of the team that gave them the job in the first place, in this specific case, siding with Republican efforts to gerrymander legislative districts.

If we could ensure that districts were created in order to make the general election competitive, politicians would have to be more bipartisan, more productive, and more focused on policy outcomes instead of political survival simply because the voting base would change and the more people who vote, the more centrist, reasonable, and moderate the electorate becomes. But unless the Supreme Court changes its mind or we change the Constitution, gerrymandering is here to stay. Which is why reforms like mobile voting and the ideas described below are so crucial.

RANKED CHOICE VOTING

Ranked-choice voting (RCV) means that rather than just picking one candidate, you rank all of them, or your top few, and candidates get points for wherever they are on your ballot, scoring more points the closer to the top of the ballot they are listed. Whoever gets the most total points wins. (Each system is a little different but this is broadly how it works.)

RCV attempts to:

1. **MAKE ELECTIONS MORE POSITIVE.** When voters have to pick several candidates, that reduces the incentive for nasty campaigns because all candidates want to be likable enough to at least be someone's second or third choice.

2. **MAKE ELECTIONS MORE CENTRIST.** In an election between more than two candidates, an outlier can win by taking extreme positions and letting the others split the larger bloc of moderates. In fact, the winner-take-all system only encourages candidates to radicalize. With RCV, because candidates want to be on as many ballots as possible, it's much harder to be an extremist and win.

3. **REDUCE COSTS.** Rather than having runoff elections if no candidate has enough votes to exceed the threshold (in jurisdictions that have a minimum threshold), the rankings can be used to determine the winner that night.

RCV makes a lot of sense, and I have supported it both financially and politically. Just as the goal of mobile voting is to make things more centrist and easier to get done, RCV promotes centrism and consensus. Is it the solution to all of our problems? No, because if you have to physically go somewhere to vote, most people still won't do it. But it has made elections better in places like Alaska, Kansas, Maine, Nevada, Wyoming, and New York City. Combined with mobile voting, RCV moves the political inputs decisively toward the center—and that means the policy outputs move there, too.

Or, as Adam Edelman said in an NBC News article, "In many

states, some of the purported strengths of the system promised by supporters—such as a rejection of polarizing candidates—came to fruition. In Alaska, for example, where ranked-choice voting was used for the first time in the state's senate and congressional races, voters chose incumbent Senator Lisa Murkowski and Mary Peltola for those offices over more extreme candidates."[3] In other words, it works.

OPEN PRIMARIES

More Americans identify as independents than as Republicans or Democrats. According to 2022 surveys from Gallup, 41 percent of Americans identify as independents whereas both major parties each receive 28 percent.[4] That's a problem, because if the ultimate outcome of an election is predetermined by gerrymandering and if independents can't vote in primaries, they're effectively shut out of the process entirely. I can tell you that from personal experience. Because I'm an independent living in New York City, my vote never counts for anything.

So how do you increase primary turnout? One popular idea is called open primaries. Right now, in most jurisdictions, only party members can participate in primaries. With open primaries, anyone can participate. It allows independents to finally stop being disenfranchised. And it gives Republicans and Democrats the chance to cross over and vote in the other party's primary instead, which inherently serves as a moderating force against extremists.

Twenty-six states currently allow open primaries.[5] New Hampshire just requires you to decide which primary to vote in by election day. In Wyoming, voters can change their party affiliation up to fourteen days before an election, allowing voters to move around so they can participate in the primary that interests them most. Not shockingly, both parties have run bills in these states to try to eliminate open primaries.

We ran a campaign in Oregon in 2014 to change the state constitution to allow open primaries. Every institutional entity came out against us—the parties, unions, trade groups, you name it—and we got our ass kicked. While polls showed that voters liked the idea, they didn't actually show up to support it. The inconvenience of voting outweighed the potential benefit of the systemic change. On the other side, everyone with a vested interest in maintaining the status quo did show up. They had a tangible reason to make the effort.

If mobile voting had been an option, would open primaries have passed? I don't know. We lost by a lot.[6] But odds are, most people who would have voted from their phones would have supported reform. That would have at least made the election a lot closer, which would have incentivized reformers to try again. Of course, this is why the powers that be will do everything they can to block mobile voting. It not only makes it easier to lose power, but also makes it easier to pass other reforms that can further weaken the incumbents' grip on power.

THE ELECTORAL COLLEGE AND THE NATIONAL POPULAR VOTE

As recent history has reminded us, the presidential candidate who receives the most votes does not automatically move into the White House. Instead, you have to win 270 Electoral College votes. Each state has a certain number of votes based on population and, with the exception of Maine and Nebraska, the winner in that state gets all of its electoral votes.

As wise as our Founding Fathers were, the Electoral College was not one of their greatest hits. They created a buffer between the direct vote and the presidency out of fear that a tyrant could enter the scene, manipulate the people, and win. It appears they got that backwards. The closest case we have of this fear being realized, Donald Trump, who lost the popular vote in 2016 and only won the election because of the Electoral College. Not only did the Electoral College fail to prevent the exact scenario the Founding Fathers were afraid of, but it has the unforeseen consequence of concentrating the presidential election in just a handful of swing states.

Right now, swing states like Arizona, Florida, Georgia, Michigan, Nevada, New Hampshire, North Carolina, Pennsylvania, and Wisconsin receive the vast majority of attention and resources in the general election. The remaining states are assumed to already be in the bag for either the Democratic or Republican candidate. For those of us living in non-swing states, that means our needs, issues, and priorities are ignored, while that handful of swing states receives priority.

This leads to ridiculous distortions, such as the federal mandate that every gallon of gas in the United States contains a certain amount of ethanol. This wasn't done because it's good for the environment or because it's necessary to make your car run. It exists because:

1. Ethanol comes from corn;
2. They grow a lot of corn in Iowa; and
3. Iowa is often the first state to hold its nominating contest for presidential elections, so whichever candidate wins the Iowa

caucus often generates the momentum they need to win the rest of the primaries.

As a result, both parties have agreed to bribe Iowa corn farmers.

We have now held five presidential elections where the person who took the oath of office was not the leading vote-getter. Most of us know that Hillary Clinton won more votes than Donald Trump in 2016. In 2000, Al Gore won the popular vote but, thanks to a controversial Supreme Court decision, lost the Electoral College vote to George W. Bush. The same thing happened to Andrew Jackson, who lost to John Quincy Adams in 1824, to Samuel Tilden, who lost in 1876 to Rutherford B. Hayes, and to Grover Cleveland in 1888, who lost the Electoral College vote to Benjamin Harrison.

If this feels unfair and undemocratic, that's because it is. To fix the problem, reformers launched the national popular vote movement in 2006, which, you guessed it, says that whoever wins the most total votes wins the election, regardless of the Electoral College. Legislation has passed in sixteen states and the District of Columbia to authorize their Electoral College votes to go to whoever wins the national popular vote. That adds up to 205 Electoral College votes. If we can push that total to 270, the Electoral College's reign of terror will end. This is a great reform, but only applies to one election for one office and only to the general election, so even if it happens, it doesn't supplant the need for mobile voting.

You may have noticed that in the two recent examples of the losing candidate still winning the election, both losers were Democrats and both winners were Republicans. Not surprisingly, support for the national popular vote has all come from traditionally blue states. There are another seven states, holding sixty-nine Electoral College votes, where one chamber of the state legislature has approved the national popular vote. But some of those states—like North Carolina, Arkansas, and Oklahoma—are very unlikely to approve it anytime soon, so the Electoral College will probably haunt us for a lot longer. Here again, mobile voting is our best bet, because it increases the power of the moderate middle, which definitionally reflects the will of the majority. That's what democracy actually is.

TERM LIMITS

Term limits are a long-standing reform that is in effect in jurisdictions across the country and at all levels of government. Many governors and mayors are limited to two terms, as is the president. Many city council members and state legislators also have term limits. But Congress does not, since that would require amending the U.S. Constitution, which is virtually impossible (requiring support from two-thirds of Congress and three-quarters of the states). Many other key elected positions also lack term limits.

That must change. If the only incentive for every politician is to stay in office, then they can only make each decision solely based on their next election, usually the primary. If they know they can only stay in office for a certain amount of time, that frees them up to take more factors into account in their last term beyond just the next election, and, to the extent that they care about actually accomplishing anything, maybe they'll take a little more political risk. It's also important to put guardrails in place that don't allow politicians to evade term limits by just jumping from one office to another. Something like saying you can only serve for, say, four or six years out of every ten- or twelve-year span (starting with your first oath of office) should help stop politicians from gaming the system.

The best argument against term limits is that it empowers unelected staff who can stay in their jobs forever, ultimately making them the true decision-makers on many issues. I'm not sure that's so bad, especially if they're governed by inputs that are not solely political. To attract the best staff, I would considerably increase salaries—it's fine if they make more than their bosses—and I would put extended revolving-door provisions into place that make it impossible for them to work for or benefit from anyone they dealt with professionally for at least five years. Just as with politicians, their incentives have to be aligned properly.

FINAL FIVE

Like mobile voting, final five is one of the newer reforms to come along. Katherine Gehl, the leader of the final five movement, has an excellent essay later in this book making the case for reform. Here's how it works: all candidates from any party appear on the same primary ballot, and all voters can participate. The top five vote-getters move on to the general election, and using ranked-choice voting, the winner emerges.

The mechanism may seem slightly confusing, but the argument for final five is anything but. When we have just two candidates to choose from, each comes from the major party, and they're generally forced to adhere to the conventional positions and policies of their party. However, more people are independents than Republicans or

Democrats, and if neither party platform was sufficiently appealing to a plurality of Americans to want to sign up, why should those voters then be forced to pick candidates who have to represent the orthodoxy of their party?

Putting all of the candidates on one primary ballot and letting anyone vote in the primary means it becomes an election about ideas and policies rather than just partisan bashing. And by having five choices instead of two in the general election, the candidates again are forced to become more than mouthpieces for their parties. Even more important, when the winning candidates take office, rather than just governing to keep a small number of partisan primary voters and special interests happy, they have to think about the electorate as a whole. And what do most voters want? They just want things to get done. As we discussed earlier, if every policy output is the result of a political input, final five changes the inputs to force elected officials to actually work together and produce results.

States can permit final five voting either through legislation or ballot measures (it differs by state), and there are local movements in every state to make final five a reality. In 2020, Alaska became the first state to approve a version of final five in which the top four vote getters advance to the general election. In 2022, Nevada voters approved the concept with close to 53 percent support.[7] For a ballot measure in Nevada to become state law, it has to pass twice, so voters will take up the question again in November 2024, hopefully making Nevada the second state to adopt final five. Like ranked-choice voting, final five combined with mobile voting could be an incredibly powerful force for change.

EARLY VOTING

This one is as simple as it sounds. Voters have more time to cast their ballot and participate in the process. It still requires voters in most states to go to an actual polling place, which still makes it too inconvenient for most voters to participate. But logic dictates that if you have more time to do something, there's a greater chance you'll do it.

Early voting is one reform that has caught on in recent years, in large part thanks to efforts by election officials to find ways to make voting safe and accessible during the pandemic. (Of course, you may be wondering, why not always try to make voting more accessible?) More than 150 million votes were cast in the 2020 general election, and roughly 70 percent of those votes were cast before Election Day.[8] Guess what happened when they made it easier to vote? More people participated. I know. Shocking.

Approaching the 2022 midterm elections, Gallup asked respondents if they planned to vote before Election Day. Forty-one percent said they did (or already had).[9] Gallup's poll found that early voting was particularly popular in western states, with two-thirds of respondents saying they planned to vote early. This is likely because states like Colorado, Washington, Nevada, Oregon, Utah and California have historically been more progressive and aggressive in making voting accessible, so voters there are used to having more options. According to the poll results, more Democrats than Republicans planned to vote early, perhaps in part due to the fallout from the various insane conspiracy theories Donald Trump peddled about the 2020 election. And voters in the Midwest and on the East Coast, especially older voters, were more likely to wait until Election Day.

If adoption of early voting has worked this well, imagine the combination of early voting and mobile voting. If voters had, say, a month to cast their ballots and all they had to do was open an app and make their selections, vastly more people would participate. And what's most important isn't necessarily even more votes in federal elections. What really matters in most cases is increasing the number of votes cast in currently low-turnout primaries in state and local government, elections that determine where most of the governing actually happens.

VOTE BY MAIL

Voting by mail is one of the most significant election reforms in U.S. history. It began with absentee ballots, starting during the Civil War so that Union and Confederate soldiers could participate in elections back home. After some fits and starts, Congress eventually passed both the Uniformed and Overseas Citizens Absentee Voting Act of 1986 (UOCAVA) and the Military and Overseas Voter Empowerment Act (MOVE).

In 1978, California became the first state to allow voters to request an absentee ballot for any reason at all. In 1998, Oregon became the first state to issue all of its ballots by mail. Washington state, Colorado, and Utah soon followed. (Not coincidentally, Colorado, Oregon, Utah, and Washington were among the seven states to pilot mobile voting). California, Hawaii, Nevada, Vermont, and the District of Columbia have all also enacted automatic vote by mail, and New Jersey used vote by mail in 2020

And, overall, this method of voting is secure. Amber McReynolds, then-CEO of the National Vote at Home Institute and Charles Stewart II, the Kenan Sahin Distinguished Professor of Political Science at MIT published an op-ed that started,

"Voter fraud in the United States is exceedingly rare, with mailed ballots and otherwise. Over the past twenty years, about 250 million votes have been cast by a mail ballot nationally. The Heritage Foundation maintains an online database of election fraud cases in the United States and reports that there have been just over 1,200 cases of vote fraud of all forms, resulting in 1,100 criminal convictions, over the past twenty years. Of these, 204 involved the fraudulent use of absentee ballots; 143 resulted in criminal convictions. Let's put that data in perspective. One hundred forty-three cases of fraud using mailed ballots over the course of twenty years comes out to seven to eight cases per year nationally. It also means that across the fifty states, there has been an average of three cases per state over the twenty-year span. That is just one case per state every six or seven years. We are talking about an occurrence that translates to about 0.00006 percent of total votes cast."[10]

Opponents of mobile voting like to cite voter fraud as a major reason to not move forward. Some also like to raise the possibility that rampant fraud exists but goes undetected. Having run multiple campaigns, I can say firsthand that so much time and money is spent scrutinizing every voter and every vote that the notion that a broad, undetected conspiracy is unfolding before our eyes is absurd. Virtually none of these opponents have ever worked at a high level on electoral campaigns and know virtually nothing about politics. Voter fraud is just not an issue.*

---

*   Voter fraud has become a popular talking point among anti-mobile-voting advocates. For all of the problems that exist in this country, voter coercion is simply not one of them. It doesn't happen, and arguing it does just exposes how little our opponents actually know about government or politics.

Has voting by mail (VBM) increased turnout? Here's what MIT's Election Data and Science Lab has to say:

The scientific literature on this empirical question about turnout has been mixed. An early study of the effects of VBM on turnout in Oregon argued that its implementation had caused turnout to increase by 10 percent. However, subsequent research has had difficulty replicating these initial findings. More recent research, using a variety of quasi-experimental methods, suggest the causal effect of VBM in these states in presidential election years is around 2 percentage points, although it may be as high as 8 points in Colorado. The safest conclusion to draw is that extending VBM options increases turnout modestly in midterm and presidential elections but may increase turnout more in primaries, local elections, and special elections. This modest increase likely comes in two ways: by bringing marginal voters into the electorate and by retaining voters who might otherwise drop out of the electorate.[11]

The key point in the quote above is that voting by mail helped increase turnout in primaries, local elections, and special elections. That's where the rubber meets the road. Because of gerrymandering, primaries almost always matter far more than general elections. And because local government does most of the important stuff—making sure the traffic lights go from red to green, making sure clean water comes out of the tap, picking up the trash, running schools, parks, hospitals, mass transit systems, jails—local elections are where higher turnout matters most. In fact, while I hope to see mobile voting become available to every voter in every election, if you told me we had to start with just state and local primaries, I'd take it in a heartbeat.

Voting by mail is a wonderful reform. Anyone who wants to vote this way should be allowed to, in any state in the nation and abroad. However, it relies on a method of communication that's rapidly becoming anachronistic. How often do you check your physical mail? Once a week? Once every two weeks? Even less than that? Compare that to how often you check your phone. Once a minute? Older voters who are more comfortable using paper ballots via mail ought to be able to continue doing so in perpetuity. But if our goal is to make voting easier and to entice more people to vote, then we need to meet people where they are. Voting by phone is effectively the same thing as voting by mail, just tailored to meet the needs and preferences of a younger generation. And mobile voting is even safer than voting by mail, due to a technological advancement called end-to-end verification, which I will describe in a few chapters.

COMPULSORY VOTING

Compulsory voting is what it sounds like—you have to vote. It's not a choice. And yes, the notion of it does feel, well, un-American. But maybe not as much as you'd think. A 2020 study from the Pew Research Center found that respondents in Germany, France, and the United Kingdom favored compulsory voting by roughly a 2–1 margin, while U.S. respondents were split almost 50–50 on the issue. None of those countries require mandatory voting (although voter registration is mandatory in France, Germany, and the UK), but twenty-seven countries have laws that do mandate voting, including Australia, Singapore, Turkey, Belgium, Mexico, Brazil, Argentina, and Peru.[12]

Would compulsory voting help increase turnout in the United States? Over a two-year period, a group of twenty-seven scholars and advocates studied this question. Two of those scholars, Miles Rappaport from Harvard and Janai Nelson from the NAACP, argued in an op-ed in the *Los Angeles Times* that it would definitely help:

> *Our conclusion is that adopting universal civic-duty voting in the U.S. would have major benefits for American democracy. It would dramatically increase participation in elections. In Australia, Belgium, and Uruguay, participation rates have remained near 90 percent for the last two decades. In the 2018 midterms, the U.S. achieved a much-touted record turnout, but still only an anemic 53.4 percent of eligible voters cast their ballots; in 2014, the figure was 42 percent. Mandatory participation would also diminish the demographic skew at the ballot box. Voting rates now vary dramatically by income, education, age, and race. Although African Americans vote in higher proportions than whites when income is factored in, communities of color, especially African Americans, have faced a variety of voter suppression policies and tactics. The adoption of universal civic-duty voting could also help shift our election laws away from policies that, intentionally or not, keep some groups from the polls. It would encourage same-day registration, ending felony disenfranchisement, preregistering sixteen- and seventeen-year-olds, paid leave to vote, and expanded*

early and mail-in voting. Schools would have a strong incentive for robust civic education to prepare eighteen-year-olds to vote. Civic organizations could invest more in public education about voting, and spend less on driving voter turnout. It's even possible that political campaigns would change for the better. If everyone is voting, then everyone is listening, and candidates and parties will need to make efforts to attract broad support, rather than focusing solely on rallying their base supporters and discouraging turnout on the part of their opponents.[13]

Their argument makes sense. As they say, if everyone is voting, then everyone is listening and parties have to adapt to attract broad-based support. In other words, political inputs dictate policy outputs. Now, is compulsory voting realistic? It would be hard to achieve politically, since the same people who make the laws have little interest in risking their hold on power. But this is true of every election reform. None are ever easy. All of them require movements. And it's not like we don't require other things from citizens. You have to pay taxes. You have to show up for jury duty. You have to register for the draft.

So while forcing people to vote may seem antithetical to the American spirit, there's plenty we're already required to do. Maybe it's not impossible. It would certainly be interesting to see a state or a city try it out. It can't be worse than what we have now.

FUSION VOTING

Fusion voting is a hybrid of several of the other reforms discussed in this chapter. It means that one candidate can appear on multiple ballot lines in the same election. The theory goes that if a candidate is running on multiple lines, they have to reach out beyond their base to appeal to voters who may be willing to vote for them, but not as a candidate of either major party. Fusion voting used to be very common, but that was back in the 1800s. It mainly went away as the two-party system emerged.

The best argument for fusion voting is that it helps smaller parties qualify for ballot lines. In order for any party not named Republican or Democrat to appear on the ballot, their leaders have to collect enough signatures to make it onto the ballot and then their line has to receive enough votes to stay on the ballot. (This is designed to be punitive since people in charge don't like any forms of competition.) The number of signatures required for a minor party to qualify for the ballot differ in every state, but for example, in my home state of New York, the State Board of Elections raised the number of signatures required from 50,000 to 130,000 just before the 2020 elections. As a result, eight parties appeared on the 2018 ballot and just four in 2020.[14]

Are third parties inherently good? No. There is a very wide range of third parties in this country—the Libertarian Party, the Green Party, the Working Families Party, the Conservative Party, the Constitution Party, the Forward Party, No Labels, the Communist Party, the American Freedom Party, and dozens more. Some are extremely left wing. Some are extremely right wing. Some exist to argue for breaking up the United States. Some want recreational marijuana to be legal everywhere. They're all over the place. But their existence eats away at the vise grip the Democrats and Republicans currently hold on power. One enviable aspect of countries with parliamentary systems of government is that big and small parties are often forced to cooperate to create a ruling majority.

Fusion voting currently exists in just New York and Connecticut. Having spent several decades in and around New York politics, I've seen fusion voting work both ways. I've seen it help form coalitions that allow new ideas to move forward. And I've seen third parties turn into corrupt fiefdoms where party bosses use their ballot line to extort money and patronage from the major party candidates. Of all of the reforms on this list, it's probably the least impactful.

Imagine if all of these reforms we just reviewed—or even some of them—were implemented. It would change our country entirely. We'd have exponentially higher voter turnout. We'd get better candidates who, if they want to get reelected, have to stop all the whining and fighting and actually work together and get things done. We'd have real solutions on climate change, health care, education, immigration, gun control, and so many other issues.

Now, of course I believe that if we can only adopt one reform, it should be mobile voting. It's the only option that meets people where they are—physically, culturally, and technologically. But we're not limited to just one reform. We can have as many of the ones discussed here as we want. We just have to fight for them.

PART 3

MOBILE VOTING IS THE ANSWER

CHAPTER 7

·······························

HOW THE MOBILE VOTING
PROJECT CAME TO BE

The idea had been turning over and over in my head for a while, ever since our firm and our counterparts inside of Uber were able to mobilize millions of customers to advocate politically through the app. We got all those people to take political action—people who are usually totally disconnected from the system. We made it easy, and we gave them a reason to care. It worked. If voting were just as easy, would more people do it? And if more people voted, would that change things?

I reached the decision to create the mobile voting project with a few clear convictions. My time in government and politics ingrained in me what I have come to see as the golden rule—that every policy output is the result of a political input—so I knew exactly where I had to start. But how could I change the inputs or introduce new ones?

My time in tech taught me how comfortable people have become conducting their lives through their phones. At this point, virtually every American adult has a smartphone of some kind, so there's no better way to reach them.[1] But with voting, there's no margin for error. Any mistakes could be fatal to the whole project. So the next question was, can mobile voting be done securely?

TechCrunch Disrupt, a high-profile conference focused on breaking technology news and developments, was a big deal for me in 2017. My partner, Jordan Nof, and I had launched Tusk Venture Partners less than a year earlier, and we were still pounding the pavement, raising our first venture fund. I was being interviewed on the main stage along with Hemant Taneja, then a managing director at General Catalyst, a top venture capital fund (Hemant is now General Catalyst's CEO) and Ted Ullyot from Andreessen Horowitz. The conversation turned to politics, and I was asked about how we used the Uber app to beat the taxi industry in city after city, state after state. This is how TechCrunch reported it:

> *Asked about how startups can get their users to lobby for regulators on their behalf, as indeed Uber does, another panelist— Bradley Tusk, who has worked as a strategist for Uber and now FanDuel—said scale obviously helps but providing users with an easy way to do it is also key… Tusk added that he is now hoping to do something to fix this wider democratic problem of not enough people voting by encouraging startups to work on building secure mobile voting technology: "There's no reason why if you can advocate for Uber or FanDuel on your phone that you shouldn't be able to vote. So one of the things we're working on is creating a challenge where we will provide funding and political help for someone to come up with a platform where you can (a) vote securely and (b) preserve the anonymity of your vote."[2]*

That's how the mobile voting project was born. I was sitting on a stage in front of a big audience, and every instinct I had was telling me to keep my mouth shut about mobile voting. Sure, there were a few startups playing around with the idea. And the weird combination of jobs and experiences I'd had in both politics and tech gave me a vantage point on this issue that not many others had. And because I got lucky and took part of my fee from Uber in equity and because that bet really paid off, I now had the money to not only promote the idea but put real resources of my own behind it. I just couldn't look at the way things were going in this country and sit on my hands. So the mobile voting project came to life.

Early the next year, Sheila Nix joined us to run Tusk Philanthropies, the nonprofit we had created to take on issues we cared about, like school meals. I knew Sheila from my time in Illinois when I was deputy governor. She had then just come off two stints as chief of staff in the U.S. Senate, first for Bob Kerry, then Bill Nelson, and she also worked on the campaign for one of Obama's competitors for the U.S. Senate in 2004. After Obama won, Sheila needed a job. I was a little worried when we hired her as policy director because she seemed way more qualified than I was, but my gut feeling was that if I treated her like an equal partner rather than a subordinate, the relationship would work. It did and after I left Illinois in late 2006, Sheila succeeded me.

We stayed in touch over the years and Sheila went on to run the One Foundation for Bono and serve as Jill Biden's chief of staff during the second term of Joe Biden's vice presidency. When Sheila arrived at Tusk in early 2017, we started thinking about taking what

I had promised onstage at Disrupt and turning it into an actual campaign.

We began getting to know the players in the industry, both startups like Voatz and Democracy Live that were working on mobile voting solutions and established election companies who were wary of investing in an idea that their customers—election officials—may or may not want. Voatz had been running digital elections for student organizations and unions. So far, from all evidence, the technology was working. No one had hacked it, and Nimit Sawhney, Voatz's brilliant founder, kept doubling down on his blockchain-based approach, making the app safer and safer.

It felt like the time was right to help Nimit test his idea and his tech on a larger stage. The vast majority of election officials are extremely cautious. They are decidedly *not* interested in taking a high-profile risk on a new technology that some experts have warned can never work. But there are tens of thousands of places in America that hold elections, and we knew that if we looked long and hard enough, we'd find an official willing to work with us.

Our search turned out to be longer and harder than I expected, but our luck turned on a casual conversation with Shelley Macleod, who had been my assistant on the Bloomberg mayoral campaign in 2009 and then became employee number one at my consulting firm Tusk Strategies in 2010. She helped me build our consulting practice, then left a few years later to attend business school at Wharton and later work at JP Morgan.

Eventually, she realized that what we were doing was a lot more fun than working at a megabank and rejoined us in 2017. Shelley is now the head of investment relations at Tusk Venture Partners. She grew up in West Virginia in a very political family. Her grandfather served as governor. Her mom served seven terms in the House and then was elected to the U.S. Senate in 2014, where she sits today. Her brother Moore was a state representative and ran for governor in 2024. Shelley is as connected in West Virginia politics as it gets.

I asked her if there was anyone in West Virginia we should be talking to about mobile voting. Shelley said she'd check with her mom and brother and get back to me. A few days later, she gave me a name and a phone number.

"Mac Warner. He's the secretary of state. Moore thinks he might go for something like this, because he's been looking for a solution to make it easier for troops stationed abroad to vote. Give Mac a call."

Mac had not only served in the army himself, I soon learned, but so had each of his four children. He knew firsthand how difficult it can be for soldiers deployed overseas to vote and he was deeply passionate about changing it. He ran for secretary of state, in part, to find a solution to that specific problem, which is especially prevalent in states like West Virginia that have high rates of enlistment.

It wasn't long after our introduction to Mac that we were developing a plan between the state of West Virginia, Voatz, and us to allow deployed military from two counties to participate in the upcoming March primary on their phones. (Voatz provided the technology; Mac's team ran the election; and my foundation paid for it so there were no taxpayer expenses.)

It was a mad rush to get everything ready, but on March 24, 2018, the very first mobile vote was cast in a U.S. election.[3] Election security rules are determined in the United States by each local jurisdiction, and in this case, the military was in charge since we were interacting with their members. They decided the best way to verify voters was by first taking a video of the voter and matching it against a facial recognition scan, then using their fingerprints to ensure they were who they said they were.

The experiment went well enough that Mac expanded the program that fall to allow deployed military in twenty-four counties to participate.[4] That worked too. The entire process was then audited by the National Cybersecurity Center and came back with a clean bill of health.

That first election generated positive press coverage and helped convince election officials in other jurisdictions to try it, too. In each case, Tusk Philanthropies covered the cost of administering the mobile portion of the election (typically around $150,000 per jurisdiction). We didn't tell the jurisdiction which vendor to use (as long as it worked, it didn't matter to us), so those who wanted to use blockchain usually went with Voatz and those who preferred a cloud solution chose Democracy Live.

Over the next few years, we sponsored twenty-one elections in Utah, Colorado, Washington, Oregon, South Carolina, Virginia, and West Virginia where either deployed military, people with disabilities, or both participated via their phones. In every case, the National Cybersecurity Center audited the election, and in every case, the election came back clean.[*] Turnout, on average, more than doubled, even with virtually no marketing effort to convince people to participate. The County of Denver conducted a poll afterward,

---

[*]   The first election in West Virginia was audited by the Blockchain Trust Accelerator.

and not shockingly, 100 percent of survey respondents said they wanted to use mobile voting in all elections in the future.[5]

After President Biden was elected, Sheila returned to government to serve as chief of staff to the Secretary of Education, and we were very fortunate to recruit Jocelyn Bucaro to join us and run the mobile voting project. We met Jocelyn when she was the director of elections for the City of Denver; it was her idea to poll the voters who participated. She was, and is, a superstar in the election space, having won four awards from the National Association of Elected Officials. Mobile voting is new and high profile, and if an election official tries it and something goes wrong, they immediately face major criticism from both parties. If they just maintain the status quo, no matter how bad it is, they're much less likely to be attacked for their choices. But there are always a few exceptions with the vision and courage to act. Jocelyn was one of those who instantly grasped mobile voting's vast potential for fixing our democracy. She was willing to put her time, her reputation, and her career on the line to try to make it happen.

The process of administering the first group of mobile voting elections went really well. The technology worked for voters. Everything ran smoothly for election officials. There was a single hacking attempt in the second West Virginia election, but it failed. Despite almost no marketing or promotion, turnout increased. People from both the military and the disability communities were really happy.

You'd think that this kind of success would open doors—that elected officials or people who administer elections in other jurisdictions would want those same results. But they don't. You can't be an elected official and admit publicly that you don't want more people to vote. Even in states like Texas and Georgia where state legislators have severely restricted voting rights, no one actually says, "We don't want more Black people to vote because they vote for the Democrats." They can only resort to euphemisms like "security" and "integrity."

Unfortunately, many within both the election reform community and academia gladly (though perhaps unwittingly) did the dirty work for them. Our opposition came from two camps: paper ballot acolytes and cybersecurity professors. The paper ballot types are a little like the anti-vaxxers. They feel like if they can keep the world locked down in some previous era, everything will be safe and secure (even if far fewer people had rights or access in the longed-for era). If you try to talk to them about, say, the problems paper ballots posed in Florida in the 2000 presidential election, they look at you like you've gone mad.

For those who don't remember, the results of the presidential election between Al Gore and George W. Bush were held up for weeks by a vote tally in Florida that was too close to call. Election officials had to recount paper ballots by hand and get judicial rulings on dealing with anomalies like a "hanging chad"—when the little piece of paper that is not fully punched out to indicate the vote is still *hanging* there. Such absurdities were how one of the most important elections in recent American history was decided, an election that was eventually decided by the Supreme Court and installed a president who responded to 9/11 by putting us into a long and pointless war. Is this the golden era that paper-ballot zealots want to enshrine for all time? I guess so.

The other group that opposes us—the academics—are easier

to understand. They are a ready-made opposition force. This is how it works: a reporter for the *New York Times* or the *Wall Street Journal* is writing a story about mobile voting and they need to make it appear balanced. The formula goes like this—"Advocates argue that mobile voting can significantly improve turnout, but security experts worry it's not safe." A computer science professor with a prestigious résumé is emailed by the reporter. If he's like most of his peers, he really, really wants to be quoted in that story. Maybe because it will impress his department chair or the college president or his mom or, who knows, maybe all three. These days, attention is everything. But there's only one role available here. The reporter needs the professor to criticize the idea. After all, he already has quotes from supporters. Now he needs the opposite. So the professor obliges and everybody is happy. It's hard to blame them for saying whatever it takes to get attention; that's human nature for far too many of us.

As many times as this charade has been played over and over, it retains formidable power. The public is impressed by academic credentials. If a professor from Harvard or Penn State or UCLA says, "Be careful, this mobile voting thing could blow up the world," that has an impact. It gives perfect cover to politicians who really don't want mobile voting but also would prefer not to be seen as obstructionists blocking the path to a more accessible democracy. Much safer to let the academics do the bad-mouthing for them.

We've polled the issue of mobile voting both locally and nationally. The data is clear: if people think that they can vote securely on their phones, they want to do it. Who wouldn't? But if they think the technology is vulnerable to hacking, they'll opt for the status quo.

Based on the polling, we knew what we had to do. We had to prove that mobile voting technology could be even safer than paper ballots or voting machines. That meant investing heavily to build the best, most secure voting technology anyone had ever seen. And from our research, we learned that the best way to do this used a game-changing technology—end-to-end verification—that even our critics admitted could be adapted to voting.

There's a lot about end-to-end verification in the tech build chapter, but put simply, it gives voters the ability to verify their ballot is recorded and cast correctly and nothing tampered with their vote. But bringing end-to-end verification to voting was not going to be easy.

The question was who would build it. You need some of the world's best cryptographers, and they don't come cheap. The government wasn't going to invest, because they don't want change in the first place. Election administration companies don't make the kind of money to invest eight figures in an R & D project that their customers may never ask for. Startups and venture capitalists don't focus on the space because the election business is known to be too small, too dispersed, too loaded with pitfalls. In theory, the major philanthropists focused on democracy reform could support it, but most of them are scared off by the criticism in the press. Nobody trusts those naysaying academics more than they do.

That left us with one option—build secure, end-to-end verifiable mobile-voting technology ourselves. And that's exactly what we did.

CHAPTER 8

....

THE PEOPLE WHO HATE
MOBILE VOTING

(And Who Really Like Things the Way They Are)

n an ideal world, once we proved that the tech works, Americans, by the millions, would jump on board with the concept of mobile voting. Unfortunately, our politics are anything but ideal. In the next chapter, we'll explain exactly how our mobile voting technology works. Before we get into all of the details, I thought it would be helpful to see the criticism—some valid, some not—we've received to date from some academics, paper ballot acolytes, and various elites. It should provide context to explain why we are building the tech the way we are.

The real opposition to mobile voting will ultimately come from the political world. It'll come from incumbent elected officials from both parties at every level of government. From lobbyists. Industry associations. Special interests. Influential third parties. Basically, from anyone who benefits from our current screwed-up system.

Unfortunately, there's another layer of opposition that the political class will hide behind. I'm not sure if these opponents even realize they're being used. These opponents tend to fall into two camps: those who believe that no matter what we do, internet voting is just too insecure and can never be trusted; and those who are just out of touch with technology, society, and pretty much anyone under the age of seventy-three.

Let's start with the true believers—those who are confident that mobile voting can never be secure. These are largely computer science professors who, based on academic or other reasons, have staked their careers on the idea that voting on a secured, mobile device is impossible.

Although I believe that they are self-interested and wrong, I have a hard time hating the academics because their opposition, while shortsighted, misplaced, and dangerous, is probably well-intentioned. The internet is a scary place. There are many scammers, and if the 2016 election taught us anything, it's that the most well-funded hackers in the world (foreign governments) are deeply interested in impacting the outcome of our presidential elections. There is a lot at stake.

I agree the internet needs a tremendous amount of regulation and reform—from eliminating the liability protections for platforms for the content posted by its users (Section 230) to a national framework for data privacy to much stronger antitrust laws and enforcement against big tech companies. However, it's also clear that so many digital services we obtain and use today, from banking to health care to transportation to dating, have become safe and reliable. We wouldn't use them if they weren't. We're able to transfer money or pay bills safely without having to worry. We're able to order prescriptions and talk to our doctors without having to worry. We're able to order taxis, buy plane tickets, and scan our entry for the subway without having to worry. We're able to meet other people who may become friends or romantic interests without having to worry.

So where does voting fit into all of this? There are two ways to look at it.

The first is that when you ask people to honestly list their priorities, being able to move money, order an Uber, find someone to date, or get a new prescription are all a lot more important to them than voting. If that weren't the case, turnout would be exponentially higher, and we wouldn't need mobile voting in the first place. If you're a hacker, you want to go to where the money is. That's not voting. Megabanks have spent hundreds of millions to ensure that online banking is extremely safe. If the banks can protect our money online, we can definitely protect people's votes during the few times a year they're cast.

The second is that because elections determine who wins power, they may be highly attractive targets for foreign governments and organizations that hate the United States, whether China, Russia, North Korea, Iran, ISIS, or half a dozen others. That's a very valid concern, and honestly, it is the only legitimate argument against mobile voting.

However, we are funding the most sophisticated, advanced, secure voting technology ever constructed. It is being built and reviewed by election security experts who are well aware of the concerns and criticisms from some of their colleagues and took all of those into account. It's why we have spent so much time and money building the tech.

But let's be fair to the critics and take their top ten concerns, one by one:

1. **BALLOT SECRECY.** In this argument, our critics are concerned that ballot anonymity could become non-anonymized at some point in the process. We are committed to ballot secrecy too, more so than our opponents, who are willing to require disabled and overseas voters to give up their privacy in order to vote in elections today. Our system protects the secrecy of every ballot by keeping ballots encrypted.

2. **BLOCKCHAIN CAN'T BE TRUSTED.** This one is easy. Our tech isn't built on blockchain and doesn't use it in any way. We also built in multiple auditing features, including checking your ballot, verifying it, and tracking it. The ability to audit is a key feature of our technology. In our testing, we have seen much greater utilization of these features than experts have expected. But instead of relying only on election officials to audit ballots to verify the integrity of the election outcome, our technology allows voters to audit their own ballots to ensure they are recorded and counted correctly, and it enables the public to audit the system to ensure there is no tampering. If any part of the system was compromised, it would not affect the integrity of the election.

3. **SECURITY ON INDIVIDUAL DEVICES AND NETWORKS IS TOO INSECURE.** Apple and Google offer various components that can be used to check integrity and help determine whether an application has been compromised. These tools can help repel most attacks. Our technology was designed to ensure that even if the device is compromised, voters' ballots are safe by giving voters tools to independently verify they are recorded and cast correctly. This level of verifiability is not available in

mail-in ballots now. This is another area where the new technology is a significant improvement on the status quo.

4. **END-TO-END VERIFICATION MAKES THE TECH TOO DIFFICULT TO USE.** We have provided demonstrations to multiple election officials and conducted multiple live mock elections. Election officials and voters both found the technology intuitive and easy to use. And in our mock elections, 55 percent of participants on average completed the Benaloh challenge when only a tiny fraction is needed to determine if any tampering occurred.[1]

5. **VOTER COERCION.** I hear this one from tech people, most of whom have never bothered to vote in a single election and know less than most toddlers about politics. "Someone could hold a gun to a voter's head while they're voting on their phone and you'd never know." First of all, if this were true, we'd have already seen it with mail-in ballots. There are zero reports of this ever happening. Second, what world are they living in? People who are desperate enough to threaten murder are mainly concerned with city council primaries? Russia's Vladimir Putin is going to send millions of hit men to the United States to hold a gun to each voter's head? This is an asinine concern.

6. **VOTE SELLING.** This bookends with voter coercion. If there were a market to sell votes, it'd already be happening for in-person and mail-in ballots. Why would selling a vote through an online ballot be any different from selling a vote on a mail-in ballot or at a voting machine? The problem isn't that votes are so desirable that there's a deep market for them. The problem is the opposite—voting is seen as too inconvenient to bother

with. In other words, there is no market for election rigging except at scale, which the voter secrecy feature of our technology prevents.

7. **INTELLECTUAL PROPERTY.** This argument came up a lot during the pilot elections we funded. Voatz, one of the two companies we worked with, wanted to protect their intellectual property and not let experts look at their code. They're a private company. If there were no such thing as protected intellectual property, nothing would ever be invented. However, this is no longer a concern. Our code will be open for review by experts and we are happy to set up appointments. Have at it.

8. **INTERNET VOTING WON'T INCREASE TURNOUT, SO IT ISN'T WORTH THE RISK.** To me, this flies in the face of all logic. The people peddling this myth are the same people who told us Uber would never get off the ground. That no one would take their driving directions from a phone. That no one would pay their bills from a phone. That no one would order groceries from a phone. That no one would enter their credit card information to buy everything from paper towels to automobiles. These people are the modern-day equivalent of medical quacks from the second century who thought leeching was a miracle cure. There are always going to be people who say no to every new thing, regardless of the merits. Letting them govern our lives gets us nowhere. If you don't believe me, ask the families of the 232,000 people who died from refusing to take the COVID-19 vaccine, because this position is essentially the same thing.[2]

9. **MOBILE VOTING WILL DISENFRANCHISE VOTERS OR EXACERBATE DEMOGRAPHIC DISPARITIES.** This is another

concern from people who live outside of reality. Social justice leaders strongly disagree as you'll see in essays by Martin Luther King III and Mark Riccobono, president of the National Federation for the Blind, in the next section of this book. Whether it's deployed military or people with disabilities or people in rural areas or voters of color or college voters away from home or any other category, giving people more options is better than leaving them with fewer. Keep in mind, no one is arguing that we should replace or eliminate the current methods of voting. For people who are more comfortable doing it that way, please keep it up. We're just talking about providing an additional option.

Mobile voting doesn't need to be perfect. It does need to be as secure as the other ways we currently vote—paper ballots and voting machines.

Both of those methods are flawed. Nowhere near the kind of research or money or attention has been paid to their security as it has to mobile voting. If we want to make perfection the standard, we need to get rid of *every form of voting*.

At a certain point, if the only two things a government can do are either fight and accomplish nothing or pass legislation only supported by political extremes, government ceases to be useful.

One way to change that is by fixing the political inputs so we can rediscover cooperation and bipartisanship. That only happens through reforms adopted at scale, like mobile voting. The other way is to decide that what's good for Texas simply isn't for Massachusetts. What's good for Mississippi simply isn't for Oregon. What's good for Utah isn't for Michigan. And in that mindset, the only solution is a national divorce.

If we truly were of two minds about everything, a divorce might make sense. If half the country truly believed that abortion was an inherent right and the other believed it was murder; if half the country wanted to end all immigration and the other half wanted to let anyone in, anytime; if half the country wanted to confiscate every gun and the other half wanted everyone to be armed at all times; if half the country believed that climate change is a hoax and the other half wanted to eliminate all fossil fuels tomorrow, then you know what? We probably shouldn't stay together.

And while the experts will tell us to wait, just wait, and wait some more until they decide it's the right time to use mobile voting, the country is falling apart as you read this. We can't afford to wait. And we can't count on the experts to ever take action. That's not what they do. They just talk. And talk. And talk. They don't even know how to accomplish anything tangible in the real world.

We tried. I funded a group of academics and experts at Cal Berkeley's public policy school to develop standards for mobile voting. The idea was to get their views on what the tech should look like and then build the tech to those specifications. It never got off the ground. The group couldn't agree on anything. They made Congress look functional. Their only conclusion was that they couldn't reach a conclusion.

Some members of the working group believe that any new method of voting is too risky and that to protect the integrity of elections, only paper ballots should be allowed. There are a few problems with their argument.

Remember the phrase "hanging chad?" Let's revisit the 2000 presidential election example to show how paper ballots have directly impacted our politics, but imagine that the outcome wasn't determined by flawed paper ballots and Al Gore won the election instead. In this scenario, 9/11 still happens. In this scenario, the nation is still attacked by terrorists who slammed planes into the Twin Towers and the Pentagon. The people who carried out the attacks—al-Qaeda members led by Osama bin Laden—are still the perpetrators. But Florida either used a better method of voting than paper ballots or the Supreme Court ruled in favor of Gore— take your pick. Either way, now President Al Gore is tasked with responding to 9/11 instead of President Bush.

As we know, the Bush administration created a false narrative that the attacks were ordered by Iraqi dictator Saddam Hussein. They then went on to argue that Hussein controlled weapons of mass destruction that he was planning to use against America. The only way to save our country was to invade Iraq, take out Hussein, and disable his nuclear weapons.

So we did. The United States military invaded Iraq in March 2003 and stayed until 2011. Over one million American men and women were sent to Iraq to risk their lives.[3] The United States used its global influence to get other countries to invade too, including the United Kingdom, Australia, and Poland. Here's what happened:

- There are a range of estimates as to how many Iraqis died in the war. The low end is roughly 100,000.[4] The high end is a little over a million.[5] So at best, imagine filling a football stadium twice over and murdering everyone in it. At worst, that stadium is filled closer to twenty times over. Either way, an incredible number of innocent people died for no reason whatsoever.

- According to the U.S. Department of Defense, 4,431 Americans also died in the war—more than the total number of people who died on 9/11.[6]

- According to the Watson Institute for International and Public Affairs at Brown University, the Iraq War cost U.S. taxpayers $1.7 trillion.[7] Let me say that again. $1.7 trillion. That amount of money could provide school meals for every kid in America for almost the next fifty years. It's the equivalent of over $5,500 for every single American. What would you rather have—$5,500 or the blood of hundreds of thousands of innocent people on your hands? Thought so.

- But here's the kicker: the 9/11 Commission then determined that Iraq *had nothing to do with 9/11.*[8] We killed somewhere between 100,000 and a million innocent people. We wasted nearly $2 trillion. The Commission found *no credible evidence* that Iraq assisted al-Qaeda in preparing or carrying out the attacks. Whether the Bush administration knew they were lying the whole time and hoped they'd get away with it or whether they just misunderstood the entire situation, it's among the greatest mistakes in history.

Would President Al Gore have made the same mistake? Probably not. Unlike key members of Team Bush, most notably Vice President

Dick Cheney, Gore didn't have ties to the American companies like Halliburton that made tens of billions of dollars from the war and the subsequent rebuilding effort. Even if Gore was just as biased as Bush, he wouldn't have had his top advisors pushing aggressively to invade Iraq, and he wouldn't have taken the political risk of fabricating evidence about Iraq having weapons of mass destruction.

In other words, paper ballots led directly to the election of George W. Bush and therefore indirectly to the false and immoral war in Iraq and endless casualties. They obviously didn't cause Bush to lie or to falsely invade Iraq. But without paper ballots, Bush would never have been president. And since the argument used by the paper-ballot-only proponents is that their method is the only safe way to vote, this disqualifies their argument completely.

Insisting on paper ballots is like using a horse and buggy instead of cars, leeching instead of actual medicine, a barter system instead of currency. It's as if the paper-ballot advocates have missed the entire digital revolution. It's as if they've never heard of or used an iPhone or a computer. Or more likely, they have and they know that if we could vote on our phones, far more people would vote and many more young people would vote. It means things would change. They can't be dumb enough to not realize that, so the only logical conclusion is that they are insisting on an outdated, anachronistic form of voting to preserve the status quo.

Paper ballots are not reform. They're the red herring used by the status quo to preserve the status quo and prevent reform.

Along those lines, let's address a second set of opponents—the "policy experts" who think that only paper ballots should be used, groups like Verified Voting.

Here's who we're talking about: people who mainly grew up in privilege. Typically went to Ivy League universities. Truly believe that intelligence, as they define it, separates the good people from the bad people. They haven't generally worked on electoral campaigns at high levels. They've never run the operations of a city or state agency like a parks or sanitation department. They haven't run anything significant in the private sector. They haven't had to make payroll.

These are the people who have never lived anywhere but the ivory tower. And here's the dirty truth: they don't want mobile voting because they don't really want you to vote. In their view, most people are too stupid to vote. Only the elite, only the highly educated, only the highly privileged should cast a ballot, and the harder it is, the more that naturally excludes the great unwashed. These are the people whose attitudes ultimately produced the backlash that produced the Trump presidency. These are the people whose attitudes ultimately made Fox News a viable business model. These are the people who pride themselves on being "progressive," but then they oppose reforms that would build affordable housing or allow charter schools in their neighborhoods. These are not the only people ruining our country, but they're certainly part of it.

Take a look at the bios of the board members and leaders of Verified Voting,[9] our most vocal opponent (Citizen Action and Public Citizen are also very agitated; it's more than a little ironic that groups who put the word *citizen* in their name are doing everything possible to prevent most citizens from voting). They have incredible pedigrees. They went to highly ranked schools. Their bios are littered with prestigious accomplishments and awards. But barely any of them have any meaningful experience in government or working on actual political campaigns.

None of that makes them bad people. I truly don't think that groups like Verified Voting and Citizen Action are deliberately subverting democracy, deliberately allowing the planet to warm, deliberately allowing school shootings to continue unabated.

Whether they realize they're being used by the status quo to maintain the status quo is unclear. And whether they realize that they're subjecting you to a much worse life solely so they can get quoted on NPR or get invited to more cocktail parties is also unclear. Either way, they're destroying our future. Don't let them.

CHAPTER 9

....

THE TECH BUILD

A note to you, the reader:

In this chapter, you'll notice a slight change in style. The content is far more technical and detailed. There are charts and graphs. We get into the nitty-gritty of each component of mobile voting and how the tech really works. Less politics here, much more cryptography. Some of you will be fascinated, I hope. Others may have a hard time getting through it.

Here's why I still chose to do it this way: our toughest opposition, as you've read, will come from the political establishment, which does not want to do anything that could reduce its grip on power. That's been a major theme of this book. But our initial opposition will come from academics and policy "experts" who oppose mobile voting because they are committed to defending the position that nothing but hand-marked paper ballots can ever be safe enough to work—the people you just read about in chapter 8. If they can convince you that mobile voting is unsafe, then the politicians never need to do anything but hide behind the academics and use them as an excuse to maintain the status quo.

So, consider what follows in this chapter to be my answer to all existing critics of mobile voting and a preemptive strike against those who will surely emerge in the future. The system we have designed works better and is safer than the status quo, full stop. We have done our homework. Here it is.

WHAT LED TO THE TECH BUILD

It was 2020. We—those of us working on the Mobile Voting Project—had funded mobile voting pilots in seven states. They all worked. But we still faced tremendous opposition from academics and think-tank types. And politicians in both parties were unquestionably going to exploit that opposition to reject mobile voting. The only way to overcome their objections, the only way to give those of us who want a better system and a better world a fighting chance, was by building something so advanced, so sophisticated, and so secure that when the critics still said it wasn't good enough, we could demonstrably show that they were wrong. So I put my money where my mouth is—$10 million of my own money into a project to build new mobile-voting technology.

The Mobile Voting Project is a philanthropic venture. I don't own the rights to the technology we are building. We transferred it to a newly formed, independent public charity called the Free Democracy Foundation. We won't profit from the gains. No one will. With that said, there probably aren't many gains to be had anyway, given the lack of financial success most voting technology companies face, plus our technology will be free to use anyway.

Part of the reason our democracy struggles is the netherworld our elections reside in. Governments don't actually create the technology to administer elections. Private companies do. But the election business is a pretty bad one. You're competing for low-cost government contracts at the whim of bureaucrats. You're under attack from whatever party isn't happy with how a particular election turned out, as well as the litany of reporters seeking conflict and experts seeking attention. If your goal is to make a lot of money and work with the absolute best and brightest, that's not happening in the elections business.

As a result, the government is forced to buy from companies with limited ability to pay employees well, limited ability to attract talent, and because of a total reliance on winning requests for proposals, a lack of innovation, risk tolerance, or willingness to fight for something better. The same limitations that frequently hamstring governments from attracting top talent plague the voting companies too. So we get poorly designed and constructed voting machines that don't work as well as they should. We get paper ballots whose results can't be properly scanned. (More on that later, too.)

When I committed the money to build and support new technology (in addition to the millions I've already spent on funding pilot mobile-voting elections), I did so with the full knowledge that success was not guaranteed. The software might not work as well as it had to. Or it might work, but no one would adopt it, for all the reasons we've been talking about.

To my great relief and satisfaction, I now know that the tech works. But the latter risk—powerful politicians and their unwitting accomplices in the academic and policy worlds—is still very real. Which is why I wrote this book. I needed to convince people—starting with you and many, many more—to take up the cause, call bullshit on the status quo, and save our democracy.

The code we developed will be completely free for use in public elections, transparent, and subject to scrutiny. We welcome all contributions and useful critiques of our work so that this technology can be the smartest and most secure the world has ever seen. My hope is that other people will review what we've built and build on it in the future—people who have something to add and genuinely want to improve democracy (both in the United States and in other countries). We know there's a balance between the risks and rewards of being transparent, but my only goal with this project has ever been to make it widely available to election officials for free and for other people who care to make the technology even better.

By 2020, we had received a clean bill of health from the National Cybersecurity Center for each of our twenty-one pilot programs that used technology from tech companies Voatz or Democracy Live.* The audits found there to have been no successful interference or attack on the election system, after reviewing internal and external security logs, processes, and procedures. In other words, it worked.

At that time, Democracy Live was the largest provider of cloud- and tablet-based voting technologies in the United States, used in more than 1,000 elections covering nearly 600 jurisdictions. Their platform for delivering and returning electronic ballots via an online portal is hosted on Amazon's cloud. Ballots are encrypted and stored in the cloud until they are downloaded and printed by

---

* The first audit was performed by the Blockchain Trust Accelerator.

the respective election administrators. The printed ballots are then scanned and tabulated like any other paper ballots.

But after all this encouragement, and even after demonstrating proof of concept at the local level, the question remained: Could it scale?

The technology we had used in our pilots presented an acceptable level of risk for elections in which only a smaller number of voters like UOCAVA (Uniformed and Overseas Citizens Absentee Voting Act of 1986) voters or voters with disabilities were eligible to participate. If more voters became eligible, which is the entire point, we needed to offer technology that provided a much higher level of protection from cybersecurity risk. And that meant end-to-end verification.

WHY END-TO-END VERIFICATION IS SO IMPORTANT

Through running our pilots, we learned two very important facts firsthand—the available technology was limited because it was closed source and didn't offer end-to-end verifiability (E2E-V). Most of the available mobile-voting technologies are owned by private companies, which means they, understandably, want to protect their intellectual property. That means the code is closed source and not open to outside review. You can't expect a private company to give away its secrets, but not having an open-source, transparent system also meant mobile voting could never scale because no one outside the vendors could validate the security.

Additionally, the Voatz and Democracy Live systems that election officials used in the pilots we funded were very advanced for the resources they had to work with, but they didn't provide E2E-V.

We knew that this would be the main technological feature we'd have to build.

E2E-V describes any voting system that uses advanced cryptography to secure votes while giving each voter the ability to independently verify their ballot is recorded, cast, and counted correctly, ensuring no attack can go undetected. In plain English, this means that E2E-V technology protects votes at every stage of the process while giving voters evidence that their ballots are properly cast and counted. This technology far exceeds the security of in-person voting. The most comprehensive study to date of E2E-V internet voting systems was conducted in 2015 through the U.S. Vote Foundation, an independent nonprofit dedicated to election integrity. In this study, titled "The Future of Voting: End-to-End Verifiable Internet Voting Specification and Feasibility Study,"[1] and conducted by a group of academic, election, cryptographic, and scientific experts, E2E-V is defined as enabling voters to:

- Check that the system recorded their votes correctly (as intended).

- Check that their votes were received correctly (as cast).

- Check that the system included their votes in the final tally.

But E2E-V can not only verify the end results of a vote; it can also provide auditable evidence of how the vote got there. This is important to prove that entire elections are secure. The cryptographic evidence ensures not only that threats are detectable, but also that if an attack occurs, it cannot have an undetectable effect on the outcome of the election.

How? Say you're a voter casting a ballot in person. In most jurisdictions, voters hand-mark their paper ballots and then scan them in equipment that contains software to read and tally the votes located inside the polling place. Their original paper ballot is retained in a secured ballot box, but voters cannot verify how the system is tallying their votes.

After the election, auditors can hand-tally the paper ballot votes and compare them to the tally generated by the scanner's software. If there is any problem with the software-generated tally, the hand-counted audit will reveal it, thus helping prevent any outside attack from successfully altering the results of an election.

In E2E-V voting systems, instead of the voter's ballot being recorded by hand on paper, it is recorded cryptographically, and the voters themselves can serve as auditors, able to make sure the cryptography correctly recorded their choices with a dedicated ballot-check feature, and confirming their encrypted ballot is included in the results. End-to-end verifiable mobile voting also provides the public evidence that the election result is correct because all activity is publicly viewable and auditable in real time. It gives the public a direct view into the election system and enables them to independently verify everything is correct.

"End-to-end verifiability," according to cybersecurity and policy expert Maurice Turner (who wrote a great essay for this book), "is the only future for mobile voting." Or, to put it another way, if you're the everyday U.S. citizen looking to make your life easier, or maybe you're Gen Z or Gen Alpha and already do everything on your phone anyway, the voting app just gave you proof you successfully participated in the democratic process. Not bad, right?

The goal of E2E-V is not just to provide correct outcomes, but to also provide tangible evidence of those correct outcomes. This makes it a critical part of the defense against anything from software bugs to security vulnerabilities and cybercrimes. Even experts who don't like mobile voting concede the benefits of end-to-end verifiability. According to Susan Greenhalgh of Free Speech for People, Susannah Goodman of Common Cause, Jeremy Epstein of the National Science Foundation, and Paul Rosenzweig of the R Street Institute, "End-to-end verifiability addresses the possibility of undetectable hacking. The results can be reliably audited for correctness, not just by election officials or vendors but by individuals or independent organizations, such as media outlets, political parties or nongovernmental organizations."[2]

It's easy to understand why end-to-end verifiability is the future of the democratic process as it evolves in the digital space.

FIGURING OUT WHAT TO BUILD

We began bringing together a coalition that included cyber experts, voting experts, national security experts, cryptography experts, the disability community, military groups, young voters, and election officials around the country. Within that coalition, we formed a committee who conducted an extensive review and request for proposal (RFP) process. Pretty soon, the right strategy became abundantly clear: we needed to build the tech from the ground up.

Our call for submissions went out on August 3, 2020. In it, we stated our goal of implementing the most security-forward-ever open-source mobile voting system with end-to-end verifiability. We wanted to find a solution that could ensure that the technology meets accessibility and convenience needs and overcomes barriers and access issues without risking the integrity of election and voter ballots.

The project would be guided by several core principles. The technology would need to be:

- A digital version of traditional absentee voting, allowing for verified electronic-ballot delivery, ballot marking, and submission of printable marked ballots as required by voting jurisdictions for eligible voters anywhere in the world.

- Easy to use and highly accessible. This means complying with the Americans with Disabilities Act (ADA) , the MOVE Act, Help America Vote Act (HAVA), Federal Voting Assistance Program (FVAP), and U.S. Election Assistance Commission (EAC) reporting requirements, as well as conforming to all various state laws and regulations.

- End-to-end verifiable, based on recommendations in the U.S. Vote Foundation's Future of Voting project.

- Transparent, with open-source components and a fully open design.

- Adhere to all widely recognized cybersecurity industry best standards, with independent third-party verifiable processes and protocols to protect voter data and system integrity (which means the various standards set by government agencies or organizations for online and mobile app security and data protection).

There was one more important piece: digital ballots would have to be able to be printed onto machine-readable paper ballots and tabulated with other paper absentee ballots. The system would have to be able to interface with ballot-on-demand and ballot printing solutions and be capable of providing a printable audit trail of tabulated votes if required by jurisdictions. Voters would also have the option of printing a plain-text version of their ballot for physical return if so desired.

And finally, the system would need to be able to resist an attack that attempted to prevent or block voters from accessing the system over a sustained period of time, otherwise known as a DDoS attack (distributed denial of service). The system would have to be able to continue correct operation during a sustained attack at a specified level—which means either a specified number of machines performing the attack or a specified amount of data being used in the attack—without slowing down by more than a certain degree.[*] These essential network configurations need to be reevaluated every election cycle to stay in pace with advancing attack technology.

Sounds simple, right? Nope. Not in the least. But fixing democracy isn't simple, either.

---

[*] The acceptable slowdown varies per election type, but as one can imagine, for a national election garnering the highest level of attack estimated at 100 gigabits per second, the system would have to be able to continue operating correctly without slowing down for more than fifteen seconds.

On September 30, 2021, we announced our two initial grantees: one to election software company Assembly Voting, and the other to a nonprofit dedicated to furthering transparency and reliability of election technology, the Open Source Election Technology Institute (OSET). Assembly Voting was given a grant to build out the encryption technology and E2E-V system. OSET was given a grant to build out an app that would meet accessibility and election standards.

Assembly Voting is a Danish company that views transparency as a key guiding principle of software development. Their election software is end-to-end verifiable down to the smallest details, while their philosophy also extends to the software they use in their technology stack, with a strong commitment to regularly engage and collaborate with key academic researchers and relevant experts in the security community at all times. Their primary technology stack consists of Linux, MariaDB, Nginx, Redis, and Ruby on Rails. Their open-source software is frequently updated and security patches are applied rapidly.

The OSET Institute shared many of the same goals and values underlying our mobile voting project—namely around accessibility and transparency in voting technology. Their team included veteran technologists with extensive hardware, software, and systems design experience from companies like Apple, Mozilla, Netscape, Google, and Sun Microsystems. OSET's mission is to research and develop election technology as a public good in order to increase the verifiability, accuracy, security, and transparency of our election systems.

Since we were undertaking a research and development project, we identified quickly that we needed additional partners to work with us on this critical mission. Over time, our team expanded to include other experts in cybersecurity, critical infrastructure, user-centered design, accessibility, and implementation to guide the work and even at times redesign or re-engineer some pieces. We were seeking to build the gold standard, to build a system so secure that it would exceed the level of security of other voting methods. For that reason, we assembled the best team to help build this technology.

That team included experts in end-to-end verifiable voting and cryptography, like Dr. Joe Kiniry and the team at Free Fair. We also engaged experts in cybersecurity and penetration testing, including Synack and HackerOne, to ensure the system was resistant to any hacking attempt. We worked closely with the National Federation of the Blind and the American Council of the Blind to continuously test the accessibility for blind and low vision users. We engaged the Center for Civic Design for guidance on the user interface and worked with the University of Colorado at Denver and AnswerLab to perform user testing with a variety of groups, including older voters, voters with cognitive and physical impairment, and even infrequent voters. And we engaged other technologists and engineers, including Formidable (now NearForm), to redesign the system as needed and based on the feedback from our user tests.

Before I tell you how and what we have built, let me first provide some context on the currently available absentee-ballot system, and how our mobile voting system compares in its security.

WHY DIGITAL BALLOTS ARE MORE SECURE THAN WHAT WE USE TODAY

In any absentee voting system, there are three voting-related elements: a local election official (LEO), a transmission element, and a voter element. In the traditional absentee-voting process, ballots and forms are transmitted by mail to and from the voter. For UOCAVA voters, federal law requires the option for them to receive their blank absentee ballot via electronic transmission over the internet, which may involve an email with accompanying PDF attachments of a blank ballot and a required absentee affidavit, or an online portal accessed through a web browser or other application using a computer, tablet, or smartphone.

For domestic voters using absentee voting, all communications between the voter and the local election office occur via the postal service. Digitizing that process meant making voting dramatically easier and more accessible for both voters and election officials. However, it only works if the mobile voting system is exceptionally secure.

To state the obvious, every single step in any voting process presents risks and vulnerabilities, ranging from human error to malicious attacks. Based on the opinions of the multiple cyber-security experts we hired to work on the tech build, all voting systems—including in-person, absentee, and mobile voting solutions—must meet six essential security objectives in order to mitigate risks, safeguard the voting system, and ensure the integrity of the election. These are:

Authentication

This is the process of identifying the voter while using the voting system. Both traditional absentee ballots and our mobile voting system rely primarily on the signature verification process to ensure only eligible voters are voting. In paper absentee voting, local election officials compare signatures on paper to reference signatures in voter registration records to ensure they match and that the correct voter submitted the ballot. (Some jurisdictions may also require additional identification, whether entered on the affidavit form or provided as an accompanying document.) In our mobile voting system, we matched this process, but we enhanced it with a one-time access code delivered by email. Because a malicious actor would need access to the voter's email to use the system, we've increased these hurdles and significantly reduced the risk of voter impersonation or fraud.

Vote secrecy

This is the process of preventing eavesdropping activities while the voter conducts voting activities. Since both absentee voting and mobile voting are conducted in an unsupervised way outside of a polling place, it is impossible to fully mitigate the risk that a voter permits others to observe how they are voting. Mobile voting introduces an added risk to the secrecy of the voter's ballot. Voters are using their own personal devices that may be infected with malware that cannot only impact the integrity of their votes but can also potentially eavesdrop on voters to view how they voted. Our technology mitigates this risk by ensuring the voting app can only be installed on devices with the latest operating environments.

By using methods such as regular code review, public vulnerability disclosure, and bug bounty programs, we can make our technology transparent, accountable, and most importantly, we can continue to make it better by bringing in experts from across the globe who are happy to review our code and offer their own ideas. Additionally, voters can disable external network connections while they are marking their ballot because the voting app does not require a live network connection during this phase, and once they are finished voting, the voting app erases all data and does not store any information related to the voter's identity or how they voted, all of which also enhances secrecy.

Vote integrity

This is the process of ensuring votes remain undamaged and unmodified. The biggest risk toward the integrity of a vote in traditional absentee voting—and even in-person voting—is human error. Inevitably, voters make errors when hand-marking a paper ballot. It happens in every election. Voters vote for more options than the contest rules permit, also known as an overvote, or they make a mistake and correct it in an ambiguous way that forces election officials to try to determine what they intended, which can and does lead to some ballots being counted incorrectly. But voters have no ability to determine if and when that happens in existing voting systems. Voters also frequently skip or miss contests altogether. (The most egregious example of this occurred in 2018 in Broward County, Florida, where the U.S. Senate race was skipped by tens of thousands of voters because they simply didn't see it.[3] The race was displayed beneath the ballot instructions on the paper ballot, and many voters missed it and did not cast a vote in the contest. It is highly possible that the election's result may have been impacted by this error.)

Our mobile voting technology eliminates the risk of these errors completely. Voters cannot make human errors on a digital device—the system will not allow them to overvote, and it alerts them multiple times if they undervote or skip a contest. And even more importantly, our technology provides voters with tools and evidence that their ballot is recorded and counted correctly. Existing absentee voting leaves voters with no way to determine if their ballot was ultimately counted correctly. With end-to-end verifiable mobile voting, voters have the tools to verify that everything is correct, giving them more evidence—and confidence—in the outcome of the election.

Vote privacy

This is the process of separating the voter's identity from the marked ballot to ensure anonymity. In traditional absentee voting, ballot privacy is maintained because ballots are kept sealed in paper envelopes while election officials complete the signature verification process. Once signatures are verified, the ballots are removed and separated from any documentation that identifies the voter. Similarly, in our system, ballots remain encrypted while election officials verify signatures. Once ballots are accepted, they are then extracted from the digital ballot box and removed to an air-gapped local network where they are mixed and then decrypted, protecting the secrecy of each voter's ballot. Air gapping will be explained later in the chapter (try to contain your excitement).

Auditability

This is the process used to ensure a vote and a voter's registration can be examined for accuracy to: (1) ensure all votes are cast as intended;

(2) ensure all votes are counted as cast; and (3) safeguard the transparency of the voting system. Auditability is similar in both traditional absentee voting and mobile voting because our system ultimately generates a printed paper ballot that is scanned and tabulated and then used in recounts and audits. But our system *enhances* that auditability through the use of the digital-ballot audit site, which displays activity logs of all of the activity inside the digital ballot box. In this way, our system is more transparent than traditional absentee voting and provides more evidence for the public to confirm the election is secure.

Service availability

This is the process of ensuring that voting resources are accessible and obtainable to voters throughout the election cycle. It's one of the biggest vulnerabilities in traditional absentee voting that is mitigated with mobile voting. Postal delivery delays and errors in both receiving one's ballot and returning it in time effectively disenfranchises thousands of voters in each election.

For example, in 2020, when only 47 percent of active-duty military and less than 8 percent of eligible citizens overseas successfully cast a ballot, a significant number of voters tried to vote but never received their absentee ballot. (This isn't just limited to military voters; I remember requesting an absentee ballot from the state of New York when I was in college and it arrived *after* Election Day. I bet this has happened to many of you too.) One-fifth of eligible active-duty military voters attempted to vote in 2020, but 43 percent of them never received a ballot in the mail, and 40 percent of eligible citizens overseas wanted or tried to vote but couldn't due to obstacles.[4]

The pandemic certainly played a role in mail-service delivery delays as well. Postal delivery standard changes over the last decade are also a contributing factor. Domestic first-class mailing standards have increased from one to three days to five to seven days in some parts of the country.* These changes in delivery rates especially affect voters who are furthest from their home precinct during an election, particularly military service members and citizens overseas.

None of that is an issue with mobile voting. On this point alone, a widely accessible mobile solution expands voter turnout. Similarly, with the expanded use of automatic vote by mail, many election officials are relying on third-party vendors to print and mail their ballots, which introduces even more risks and can lead to incorrect ballots being sent to voters. All of these issues are effectively eliminated with mobile voting.

When you consider that human error, postal delays, lost mail, insider or coordinated attacks, and even hanging chads have all influenced the outcomes of various elections, you can see that the consistency and security of our technology changes the game entirely.†

Now that you understand what's required, I'm going to tell you exactly what we have built and how we built it.

---

* The Postal Regulatory Commission performed a review of the United States Postal Service (USPS) mail servicing within fiscal year 2021 and determined that for the seventh year in a row, no first-class mail category achieved its service performance goals, and that twenty-one of their twenty-seven regulated product categories failed to meet their targets.

† For a direct comparison of how the Mobile Voting tech handles each and every threat and risk against the system, please see the appendices beginning on page 226. We created threat model charts for every step of the voting process: the absentee ballot delivery process, the ballot-marking process (where the greatest risks associated with marking are voter coercion/ vote buying or interception of a ballot by the incorrect person), marked-ballot return, returned ballot processing and tabulation, and post-election audit (where the threats and risks remain the same since both systems rely on paper ballots).

BUILDING THE TECH

The technical work began in 2021. The team spent the first eight weeks designing and scoping the project and beginning to build the threat models that would guide the security-first approach. We knew our platform and its underlying systems would have to be built with a security-focused architecture using a DevSecOps approach. DevSecOps is a modern approach to software development that puts security first and aims to build security into a system, instead of building a system and trying to secure it postproduction. That would be too late.

Because the truth is, there are no shortcuts. Building the gold standard of voting technology would present many challenges. We didn't back down from any of the obstacles we faced—or that anyone would face if they were willing to invest the time and resources to create this technology. But here are the main challenges we had to overcome.

Authorization

One of the first key design dilemmas was figuring out how to deliver an authorization token to voters without relying on either postal mail or vulnerable emails that sit in your inbox indefinitely. Our solution was a time-expiring, single-use access code delivered to the voter's email only during the time the voter is on the app.

The code is generated during the voter onboarding phase, when voters are required to input identifying information (name, date of birth, and either the last four digits of their social security number or driver's license number). That information is then used to locate voter registration records and determine whether a voter is eligible to vote in the election and to use the app. (To be clear, this is just how the system determines if a user is a registered voter who is eligible to vote, not how it actually verifies that the person using the app is the same person listed on the registration rolls.)

The voter is then prompted to verify their information is current. If updates are needed, they are directed to an external voter registration site to update either online or through a paper registration form. After the voter has confirmed their eligibility to vote, they are then prompted to select a return method. Both digital and physical ballot-return options are available in the app.

Voters are prompted to confirm their email address before the system initiates the data exchanges in the back end that trigger the delivery of a time-expiring code to the voter's email. Once the voter successfully enters the correct code into the app, the system generates the public-private key pair used to encrypt the voter's ballot on their device, and the voter is authorized to use digital ballot return.

The one-time access code process solved a lot of usability and accessibility issues. It also provides an extra level of assurance that only the eligible voter can access and cast their ballot digitally, preventing malicious actors from attempting to vote fraudulently. And it also helped us harden the system against flooding attacks, a type of attack in which threat actors attempt to disrupt the system by submitting hundreds, or even thousands, of fake ballots to either cause a denial of service attack or sow distrust in the system. After following these steps, the voter is now authorized to vote, securely, on the app.

Usability of End-to-End Verification (E2E-V)

The next problem we faced was perhaps our most challenging, and indeed is one of the most difficult aspects of building an end-to-end verifiable voting system. A common critique of E2E-V voting systems is that they are only truly verifiable if voters actually use the verification tools. We could build a system that uses advanced encryption to secure voters' ballots, but if voters do not take the extra steps to actually verify that the encryption is working and their ballots were recorded and cast correctly, how would we know if there was a successful attack that compromised the integrity of the election?

End-to-end verifiable voting systems attempt to solve this by giving voters the option to challenge their ballot again before it is committed—or cast. Some refer to this as the "Benaloh challenge," named after Microsoft senior cryptographer Josh Benaloh, who initially created the challenge in his work on end-to-end verifiable voting systems.

This challenge can take several forms, but it typically requires the voter to have some understanding of both cryptography and hashes, with the ability to copy and paste—or manually enter—long hashes with upward of forty or more characters, and then be willing to spend several extra minutes re-voting their ballot after the challenge is complete.

Sounds difficult, right? That's because it typically is. Research on the usability of the Benaloh challenge typically finds voters nearly universally do not understand the process, and consequently do not perform it. Even Assembly Voting had identified usability issues with its existing version of the Benaloh challenge. They reported that in most elections they had conducted prior to this project, very few voters conducted the challenge before submitting a ballot.

Considering this ballot-checking process is a critical requirement in E2E-V and provides the best tool to mitigate the risk that malicious actors could attempt to secretly change voters' ballots, we knew we needed to design a new and improved version.

Assembly Voting's cryptographers got to work and designed a new method that vastly improved the usability. This new version of the challenge requires voters to enter a much shorter, seven-digit alphanumeric code in an independent verification app, also referred to as the digital ballot audit site. This independent app can be set up and hosted by the local election official as well as any third-party organization—including political parties or candidates, academic institutions, issue committees, or other interested groups. It is used as the independent verifier through which voters can verify their ballots have been recorded and cast correctly, and additionally, the public can view all activity in the digital ballot box of the system.

It works like this: the initial ballot checking code, as it is named in the app, serves as an address locator, allowing the digital ballot box to locate the encrypted ballot as the first step in the challenge process. The code represents the truncated seven-character alphanumeric code version of the full forty-three characters address of the voter's ballot on the digital bulletin board. This code identifies the full address, which then validates the integrity of the voter's ballot. The risk of collision between these codes is mitigated by validating uniqueness before posting any new items on the bulletin board. The code represents an identifier, not a cryptographic key.

Also, there is a short time in which the code can be used after the ballot has been encrypted and until the voter decides to cast or spoil the ballot. Once the ballot is located, voters are then prompted to initialize the challenge and spoil the encrypted version of their ballot by tapping a button in the voting app.

This critical moment is the first time the voting app is aware that a voter is performing the challenge. This is key because it also prevents any malicious actor who may have successfully attacked the voting app—or the device the voter is voting from—to also manipulate the ballot check process.

Once the voter has tapped the button to initialize the challenge, the digital ballot box then requires them to verify an additional seven-digit pairing key that will be displayed in both the voting app and verifier, which helps confirm they are performing the check using a valid verification site. Once this pairing key is confirmed, the independent verifier displays a decrypted version of the voter's ballot as it was recorded and encrypted in the digital ballot box.

This is a crucial moment, because at this moment, voters would be able to detect if any of their vote choices had been altered, preventing an illegitimate vote from being cast. Being able to check that your ballot was entered correctly is a fundamental aspect of an end-to-end verifiable system. And secrecy is preserved because once the ballot-checking process begins, the ballot is spoiled, or effectively annulled, and once the checking process is complete, the user interface will guide the voter to cast a new vote again, ensuring their final vote is both secret and secure.

This new design for the Benaloh challenge seemed very

promising, so we tested it with voters to find out. We began hosting a series of mock elections with partner organizations, including Civics Unplugged, Turnout Activism, 18by Vote, HeadCount, and the National Federation of the Blind, who helped recruit a wide variety of voters—from first-time voters still in high school to blind voters to older voters who may have less experience with technology.

Our hope was that at least 5 percent of the voters would perform the challenge during these mock elections. You may wonder why our goal was so low, but the fact is, you only need a small minority of voters in an election to perform the challenge to be confident that if there was a widespread attack on the system, we could detect it.

We also wanted to ensure we were testing in an environment that most closely mimics a real election. None of the voters who participated in the mock elections had any prior experience with the voting app. Instead, we provided them with instructions by email that resembled the instructions a local election official would use in an actual election to communicate with voters eligible to use mobile voting. These instructions included details on how to download and install the voting app, as well as a checklist of actions the voter may want to perform, including a note about the ballot check (a.k.a. the Benaloh challenge), with a live link to the verification site.

As of the end of 2023, we have conducted five mock elections, through which a total of 400 voters have cast ballots. Of those, over *55 percent* conducted the challenge before they submitted their ballot. This figure was consistent across the five elections, ranging from as low as 40 percent to *as high as 61 percent of voters* completing the challenge. We were incredibly encouraged by this data, which far exceeded the 5 percent minimum we hoped for—and also blew away any prior data in user studies of the Benaloh challenge and end-to-end verifiable voting systems.

We knew we had met our goal of improving the usability of the challenge, but even more importantly, we now believe we have the most promising technology for end-to-end verifiable voting that proves the security of mobile voting.

Ballot Decryption

We still had another glaring obstacle: the ballots ultimately would need to be decrypted and printed onto paper ballots for tabulation, but there isn't a way to decrypt ballots safely online. This was the conflict we faced in designing a system that is end-to-end verifiable but also meets existing absentee ballot rules.

In typical E2E-V systems, the ballots never need to be decrypted. Instead, votes can be tallied in a mathematically verifiable way while encrypted to ensure not only that the votes remain secure, but also that voters are able to verify their vote was included in the final tally. While Assembly Voting's cryptographic protocol supports this approach, we knew that the system would need to be compatible with existing absentee voting processes, including paper-based tabulation.

Thus, the digital votes would need to be first decrypted, then printed and tabulated in the same way other absentee ballots are counted. But this was the problem—if the ballots are decrypted in an online setting, the decrypted votes would be vulnerable to attack and we would no longer have a way to detect it. Remember, our goal is to protect cast ballots and ensure that any threat is detectable so that, ultimately, there is no threat to the integrity of the election itself. Decrypting ballots online would have presented an unacceptable risk of an undetectable problem. But the solution proved to be simple. We took it offline.

We did this by using a security countermeasure called air-gapping (you can stop holding your breath now). An air gap is based on the idea of creating an unbreakable barrier between a digital asset and malicious actors, which could mean a hacker, a virus, or malware. As its name indicates, an air gap is accomplished by detaching a system from any type of external network, preventing remote access by anyone who may harm it intentionally or unintentionally.

Air gaps serve two key security purposes: they defend against intrusion into a network or system, but they also protect digital assets from being destroyed, accessed, or tampered with.

In most cases, these two purposes overlap, although they're actually distinct. Many cybersecurity experts view the air gap as the ultimate countermeasure to a wide range of threats, including systems and computer networks that are used in elections, due to the simple fact that a potential attacker cannot remotely harm an offline system or network and would need physical access to carry out an attack. In other words, malware from the internet cannot spread to an air-gapped system, and hackers cannot take control of an air-gapped system if they have no way of penetrating the system.

Air-gapped architecture moves processes from an automated and internet-connected state to a manual, non-internet connected state. Besides significantly lowering data-tampering vulnerability, it also reduces the potential risk of data leaking from the server and client-related components in the solution to malicious external actors. By removing the encrypted votes from the internet-connected system and placing them into an air-gapped local area, we could decrypt the ballots safely, secure from outside sources.

The only way to tamper with the ballots now would be by physically accessing the system, which is protected in the same way that all ballots are protected: by distributing a private decryption key in separate parts. Different people, known as trustees, would each have a different part of the key, and a certain threshold of these trustees would be required to decrypt the digital ballot box.

This solves two problems: it reduces the risk that a decryption key could be lost by a single person, rendering the ballots essentially invalid, and it prevents a single trustee from tampering with the digitally cast votes. Multiple trustees can check each other to ensure that the election is secure, similar to how bipartisan election officials oversee elections now.

To lock the digital ballot box before the election, all trustees must be present to generate and receive their part of the private ballot-box key. No one person will be able to generate the full key, ensuring a single person could never decrypt the ballot box alone. Each trustee keeps their part of the key on a device that will be protected with physical security measures. When it is time to decrypt the ballots, the trustees will insert their key to compute a partial decryption, and once the threshold is reached, the system will aggregate the keys and extract the results of the decrypted ballot.

Honestly, do you think anything even remotely resembling this level of security or sophistication exists for paper ballots or voting machines? Not even close. Not even by a fraction. This is

the first-of-its-kind digital emulation of how our current physical ballot boxes are locked, a process that creates digital proof
that the ballot box was correctly sealed. These security measures
are *that* essential, and a very large team of people worked incredibly hard to solve them.

And What about Design?

You're on the VoteHub app, and everything's running smoothly, so you're probably not thinking a lot about what's going on
behind the scenes. Though the challenges we faced on the user-
facing voter app design may seem less consequential on the sur-
face, they were anything but.

One unique challenge had to do with the issue that the size of a
phone screen is a lot smaller than a normal ballot. In elections where
there are long lists of candidates, what happens when your phone
screen only shows a few candidates and not the whole list? Breaking
the list up into multiple web pages—and therefore suggesting pref-
erential placement through the visual order for some candidates and
not others—is not okay, so we worked out a way for every candidate
to be listed all on one scroll before advancing to the next contest.

Given the wide array of smartphone screen sizes as well as
voters' accessible font size settings, and the potential for large contests with far more candidates than could reasonably fit on one
screen, we couldn't guarantee all candidates would be shown on
the screen at the same time. But our solution was to require that
a voter scroll through the entire contest before advancing to the
next contest, ensuring an equal degree of fairness in their choosing
a candidate as a paper ballot offers.

How It Actually Works

I'm sure you've been waiting for this! Knowing the inherent challenges we faced, you're probably wondering how it all works. It hasn't been easy, but ultimately we are building a mobile voting system that adheres to our guiding principles and the highest known level of voting security ever created.

The diagram on the following page shows the system, including the different components of the system and how they interact, from the native mobile voting app used by voters to the back-end systems used by local election officials. The following details the steps to vote in our secure system:

1. Local election officials begin by setting up an election through the election official interface. Election setup includes configuring the local rules governing the election and importing the data with ballot definitions and eligible voter registration information. All of this activity is logged and can be viewed publicly in the digital ballot audit site. .

2. Once voting is open in the election, voters use the mobile application to provide personal identifiable information that is used to verify their voter registration status. (This was described earlier: by looking up the voter registration data in the back end to confirm voters are eligible to vote in the election, have not already cast a ballot, and are eligible to use mobile voting in case local jurisdiction rules limit use to only certain groups.) This process also helps ensure the voter receives the correct ballot based on the voting district in which they live.

3. The app then presents voters with the option to print and return a

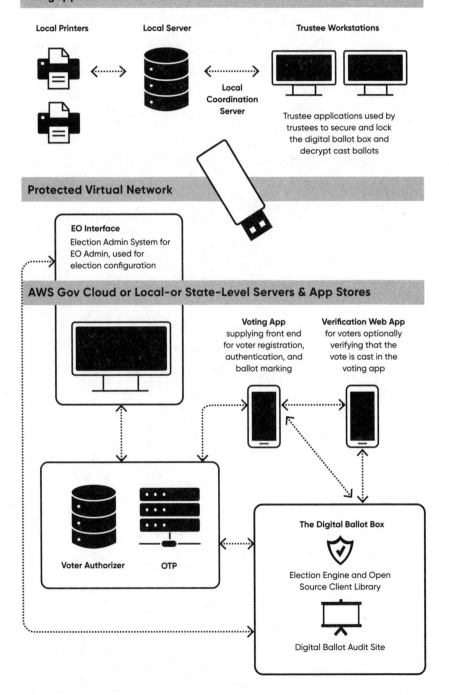

Air-gapped LAN in EO Office

Local Printers

Local Server

Local Coordination Server

Trustee Workstations

Trustee applications used by trustees to secure and lock the digital ballot box and decrypt cast ballots

Protected Virtual Network

EO Interface
Election Admin System for EO Admin, used for election configuration

AWS Gov Cloud or Local-or State-Level Servers & App Stores

Voting App
supplying front end for voter registration, authentication, and ballot marking

Verification Web App
for voters optionally verifying that the vote is cast in the voting app

Voter Authorizer   **OTP**

The Digital Ballot Box

Election Engine and Open Source Client Library

Digital Ballot Audit Site

physical ballot or to submit their ballot digitally from their mobile device. Voters who select digital return are prompted through the one-time access code process, as previously described. Voters must input this code into the voting app to receive an authorization to submit a digital ballot.

4. The voter then marks their ballot and signs their absentee affidavit. The app provides voters with notifications if they skip a contest or do not vote for all of the potential options, and it prevents them from voting for more than the available options.

5. The voter's ballot is then encrypted by the digital ballot box that uses homomorphic encryption for end-to-end verifiability (a type of encryption algorithm designed to allow important mathematical operations performed on encrypted data by converting it into ciphertext that can still be analyzed and worked on as if in its original form). The signed affidavit meanwhile is separately encrypted to protect the voter's identity and preserve the secrecy of their ballot.

6. Once the ballot is encrypted, the voter has the option to submit it immediately or perform the ballot check—the Benaloh challenge—to ensure it was recorded and encrypted correctly. Submitted ballots remain encrypted in the digital ballot box while local election officials perform signature verification on the accompanying affidavit forms.

7. Once ready for tabulation, encrypted ballots are then exported using removable media to a local area network that is air-gapped from any external network connection. As described, encrypted ballots are mixed and decrypted by a

board of trustees, each of whom maintains a portion of the decryption key.

8. Decrypted ballots are then printed onto scannable paper for tabulation according to local processes used for all other by-mail absentee ballots.

If you are the voter using the mobile application, the whole process only takes you about three to five minutes, depending on the length of the ballot.

The culmination of these system components has the security strengths of:

- End-to-end verifiability via cryptographic methods within the verification web application

- Separation of duties for election administrators, trustees, and voters

- Multiple voter authentication layers, including the use of a time-sensitive one-time access code as well as traditional absentee-ballot verification

- Digital ledger technology that ensures received ballots are not changed without detection

- Tools to detect malware on voters' devices that affects how votes are recorded

- Capability to print at home and to submit via traditional mail methods

- Threshold decryption to prevent any one person from being able to decrypt ballots

- Mixing processes that ensure votes cast are anonymized from election officials

- A publicly viewable log of all ballot transactions occurring during the election

- Audit capabilities that can cryptographically prove all legitimate cast ballots were counted

- The ability to print scannable ballots

- Adjudication platform that allows election officials to verify signatures digitally

- Air-gapped architecture that protects decrypted ballots from internet exposure

- High-availability backups of encrypted ballots

Now you know how it all works. (There will be a quiz on this later.) You can even imagine downloading and using the app. In your mind, you know it probably will take all of five minutes and you never have to leave your house or office to vote (or even got out of bed if you really didn't want to). And most importantly of all, it's secure.

Turning Every Stone

So where are we now? Drake Rambke, who has served as the project manager for building the mobile voting system, notes that trailblazing—creating what doesn't exist already—is, to put it mildly, very hard. Working with scores of security consultants, the goal was to leave no stone unturned—if someone sees a vulnerability, any vulnerability, we want it to be addressed. And when it comes to security, this covers everything from basic app identity protection to protecting against large-scale cyberwarfare.

After the first year of R & D, we felt our first iteration of the app wasn't quite yet succeeding on our goals of accessibility, particularly for usage with the blind community. We began working with another U.S. company called Formidable, who was able to solve the accessibility problem.

Having begun our design process with a thorough review of the voluntary voting system guidelines (VVSG), whose recommendations adhere to very strict accessibility standards, Formidable used these rules and recommendations as the basis for all their wire frames (design schemes), prototypes, and hi-fidelity mocks. (With clickable menus and buttons, hi-fi mocks provide a visceral sense of the user experience, allowing teams to tweak usability before final designs and testing, helping us make the app accessible for all voters from the start.)

Given the accessibility concerns particular to the smartphone, such as a voter's already-existing accessibility system preferences, use of a screen reader, and level of dexterity, it was essential to solve for each and every need, and we continue to work with external groups and disability experts to make sure we are providing the best user experience possible. We are working closely with the National Federation of the Blind to continue to foolproof the accessibility features, and we continue to get as much user testing as possible.

But know this. The Mobile Voting Project's guiding principle is to solve for security. It is being built into every aspect of the architecture, not just a feature to add in later. Remember DevSecOps? The definition is this: development, security, and operations. DevSecOps automates the integration of security at every phase of the software-development life cycle, from initial design through integration, testing, deployment, and software delivery. That's every phase, integrated into every aspect of the first-ever complete end-to-end verifiable mobile voting system that we are creating. And every feature of our approach preserves all-important voter secrecy while always remaining secure.

Take the use of multifactor authentication for voters who choose digital return: a voter with a completed ballot is processed through a second authentication flow. They initiate the authentication within the app and then are presented with a time-expiring, one-time access code via registered email address. Once authenticated, a key pair is generated: one public key and one private key, which never leave the user's device.

Another example is through the Benaloh challenge, where after encrypting a ballot, the voter has to choose whether to cast or check that particular ballot, and this decision is mutually exclusive.

If cast, that ballot will be registered in the ballot box as "cast" and will count in the tally. If checked, the ballot will be registered in the ballot box as "spoiled," and some secret information about the ballot is revealed such that the encryption can be undone and the vote in plain text can be presented to the voter.

Once the ballot is considered "spoiled" it cannot be counted in the tally, where it could be used to prove the voter's choice. So when a vote is being checked, it is effectively annulled, and the user interface guides voters to cast their vote again, resulting in a final vote that is both secret and secure. And, finally, the air-gapping technology, as described, preserves both the secrecy and security of the ballot box.

It all boils down to risk. All along, the biggest priority has always been and always will be the system's security. Cybersecurity expert Maurice Turner explains "this voting experience represents the first-ever security-first design process." This was our goal.

Building successful apps takes years. They are tested and tested, and tested again. When the security of an election is at risk, the stakes are high. The opposition will use delay tactics to avoid facing political change. They'll say we're not ready just yet. That we need to wait. That we need more testing.

We expect the public rollout and system's usage to happen incrementally, starting perhaps with state and local elections, maybe even just primaries, and maybe only for certain groups of voters. We need to continue to test and improve the product all along the way, which is also why we made it free to use and available to verify.

We can't afford not to do this. Society can't keep going this way. Our democracy won't survive decades more of dysfunction and hyperpolarization. We are in the middle of a five-alarm fire, and mobile voting is the only scalable way to solve the primary turnout problem and put the fire out.

The build of this technology has been a vast, thorough, expensive, all-encompassing process to create a security-first system that is end-to-end verifiable, and most of all open for all to test and scrutinize.

Now it's your turn to do one simple thing—help us spread the message about why it's so vital to our democratic evolution to use it. While we desperately want everyone's support for mobile voting, we think it is most likely that our greatest firepower will come from Gen Z and Gen Alpha, digitally native generations who do everything on their phones and are too sophisticated to accept excuses from the status quo as to why they can't use their phones to vote. The next two chapters explain why we have so much confidence in these generations and what they—and everyone—can do to help move our movement forward.

PART 4

PERSONAL ESSAYS

(The People Who Like Mobile Voting)

B y now, you understand the problems facing our democracy, the urgent need for mobile voting, the people who oppose it, and even the tech we've created to make this happen. But ultimately, the best arguments come from the people themselves—leaders from a wide variety of movements who all strongly support mobile voting. Here's the case for mobile voting directly in their words.

MARTIN LUTHER KING III

- *Civil rights leader*
- *Drum Major Institute chairman*
- *Former president of the Southern Christian Leadership Conference*

n 2023, we marked the sixtieth anniversary of the March on Washington and my father's "I Have a Dream" speech. The anniversary was especially poignant at this critical moment when our democracy has reached an inflection point and so much of what my father fought for is being eroded.

Rights that Americans hold dear are under assault across the country. Reproductive rights, the ability to be our full selves, and the very pillars of our democracy are growing weaker every single day. The crisis has grown so dire that my daughter enjoys fewer rights today than when she was born fifteen years ago.

It is no accident that the erosion of our civil liberties has coincided with the rolling back of voting rights in states across the country. When my father marched for equality decades ago, he understood that voting rights were a necessary part of the struggle for freedom and equality. Those on the other side know it too, which is why they have systematically made it harder for every American to vote. Eligibility requirements, polling locations, and open hours at the polls have all been manipulated to keep too many Americans from being able to vote. In my home state of Georgia, they even made it a crime to give water to people standing in line to vote.

Our voting rights should be sacred, and any effort to suppress or retract the right to vote must be stopped. My father used to say that "oppression is being legislated." It is change for the better that should be legislated, not oppression. Legislate change. Legislate hope. Not hate.

That is why my wife, Arndrea, and I are mobilizing to press for new federal voting-rights legislation to restore the right to vote not merely as an aspiration but a reality, and to guarantee that every eligible voter, regardless of race, nationality, or location, can access and cast their ballot knowing that it counts.

But we don't need to wait on Congress to act. There are efforts across the country to expand access to the ballot, including the campaign for mobile voting. Few efforts hold the potential to impact voter participation like mobile voting. Far too many voters are left out of the voting booth by existing voting options—from our military service members to voters with disabilities and even our youth. Mobile voting would empower all voters to exercise their most fundamental democratic right using the same technology they use in their everyday lives. No more waiting in hours-long lines at the polls. No harried parents carrying tired toddlers. No young students trying to balance school, work, and life while finding a way to get to the polls. And no more threats or intimidation to keep certain voters from the polls.

Why wouldn't we increase participation in elections to give everyone their chance to be heard? Why wouldn't we ease barriers on low-income voters and help hourly workers? Why wouldn't we eliminate barriers encountered by voters with disabilities who find it incredibly challenging to get to polling places on Election Day? Shouldn't they have the same right to cast a ballot as everyone else?

Every vote lost to accessibility or suppression is a loss for democracy. Increasing access is essential and to evolve through technology is a sign of the times. We already live so much of our daily lives on our smartphones—from paying our bills to accessing health care. I've been doing my banking on my phone for years, and at no time did my money go where it was not supposed to. We know there are security risks inherent in mobile voting, just as there are in other voting methods. But given how embedded mobile technology tools are in our daily lives, we also understand that risks can be mitigated. Surely the need to protect and expand access to our democracy mandates that we balance those risks and ensure every citizen can exercise their right to vote.

Every positive change is always hard won. We at the Drum Institute like to say, "Don't give up, don't give out, don't give in." My dad used to say, "A voteless people is a powerless people." And one of the most important steps we can take is that short step to the ballot box. Vote with your heart and mind, but vote in the most accessible, available way possible. Democracy depends on it.

CONGRESSMAN JOSH GOTTHEIMER

· *U.S. Representative for New Jersey's*
Fifth Congressional District
· *Co-chair of the House Problem Solvers Caucus*

One of our greatest responsibilities as Americans is voting. Democracy does not live up to its fullest potential when the majority of the voters aren't heard. Yet, despite this great gift that many around the world continue to die for, we still have a serious voter turnout and ballot access issue here in the United States.

Using the 2020 presidential election as a benchmark, the U.S. ranked thirty-first in national voter turnout compared to forty-nine other countries. Turnout in midterm elections averages 40 percent, and primary elections are even worse, with an average of 27 percent of registered voters. Not to mention, in recent years, the average turnout for local elections across the United States was less than 15 percent.

The impact of low voter turnout and participation is clear: it leads to more extreme candidates who pander to the wings of their party, and, as a result, it discourages reasonable, moderate policies, rhetoric, and governing.

Why? Right now, with only 27 percent turnout, if elected officials or candidates want to win their primary, then they have to kowtow to that small sliver of their party. That group of base party voters is customarily more dogmatic in their views and expect their candidates to take firmer positions. In other words, the low voter turnout encourages more extreme positions and creates disincentives for moderation.

The polarization and extremism are pulling our nation apart and creating nonstop gridlock in Congress. In fact, according to Pew Research Center, congressional Democrats and Republicans are further apart ideologically than at any point during the past five decades.

If more people participate in elections, including primaries and general elections, then more elected officials in Washington will have to speak to a broader population of Democrats and Republicans in their home states, and their public positions and words will have to be more bipartisan. If only a sliver of one side participates in primaries or general elections, then we are left with incredibly partisan candidates.

I represent a congressional district that is more moderate, meaning that I am always speaking to Democrats and Republicans. But I'm one of the few. Of the 435 congressional districts, only about thirty are true swing districts.

I believe that with the right tools and public awareness, we can implement solutions that will make it easier for people to vote and drive participation up in primaries and general elections. Some solutions include mobile voting, designating Election Day as a federal holiday, and expanding vote by mail and early voting.

Our country is thirsty for more reasonable, moderate governing and rhetoric. Only the Chinese and Russian governments win when we tear each other apart on social media and cable news and live in an endless swirl of gridlock. And they encourage it.

I've seen firsthand what happens when you have members willing to take the more reasonable approach. In Congress, I'm proud to co-chair the bipartisan Problem Solvers Caucus, a growing group of sixty-four members in the House, equally split between Democrats and Republicans. The group is committed to forging bipartisan cooperation on key issues facing our nation, and we do this by getting together to do the unthinkable in this day and age—finding common ground on the toughest issues facing our country. When we get to 75 percent agreement on a commonsense issue or piece of legislation, we stand and vote together as a block. That can be very influential in a narrowly divided House of 435 members. We are far better off when we work together to find bipartisan solutions.

The Problem Solvers Caucus is not perfect, and—of course—we have our policy differences, as Democrats and Republicans always do. But, I think we have discovered an old ideal that was lost along the way: trust. By working together, day in and day out, we have developed real, trusting relationships and friendships—always treating one another with respect and civility, even when we disagree.

With our bipartisan approach to governing, the Problem Solvers Caucus played a critical role during the 2023 debt-ceiling negotiations and helped pass the Bipartisan Infrastructure Bill, the Pact Act for veterans, the CHIPs and Science Act, election reform, and pandemic and historic gun-safety legislation. The evidence couldn't be clearer: working across the aisle on reasonable common-sense ideas gets things done.

The situation we find ourselves in is that the majority of the country wants bipartisan governing, yet because of polarized primaries, gerrymandered congressional districts, and low election turnout, the candidates and elected officials pander to the extremes.

I don't have the space in this forum to address every one of those issues, so I'll focus on just one that I believe is critical—voter participation in election. I believe efforts like mobile voting can effectively expand access to the ballot, involve a much broader base, and, in turn, encourage more bipartisan governing. In 2020, when vote by mail was implemented because of the pandemic, turnout was an average 5.6 percent higher in states that mailed every voter a ballot. We have even seen counties nearly double their voter turnout after offering mobile voting as an option for eligible voters. These solutions help our men and women in the military and their families vote from overseas, and help people with disabilities, tribal communities, voters living abroad, students away at school, and those experiencing unexpected emergencies cast their vote.

The logical next step is to continue to expand ballot access using new, innovative, and secure technologies and processes. It just makes sense that we work toward that goal, because it will help more people vote and, as a result, help elect more problem solvers to effectively legislate and govern.

Mobile voting won't be implemented overnight in every town, county, and state across the nation. But the bottom line is that we need to address America's ballot access and turnout deficiencies. To those who say this type of election reform is impossible, just look at the Electoral Count Reform Act, bipartisan legislation I introduced in the House and Senate and signed into law. The Problem Solvers Caucus helped get that legislation across the finish line to reform the process by which the electoral votes are counted in each state, to clarify the role of the vice president, and help avoid another fiasco like the one that led up to January 6.

We must work to do everything we can to ensure that all Americans are voting in local, state, and federal elections because voter participation is the backbone of our democracy.

MAURICE TURNER

· Public Interest Technologist and
Election Security Expert

consider myself to be a public interest technologist. It is a straightforward way of saying that I have spent my career forever optimistic about the promise of new technologies while struggling to help deliver those promises in an equitable way. The ability to translate effectively between technology innovators and policy stakeholders has provided me with the opportunity to work on unique projects including public sector IT modernization and broadband internet access for underserved communities. But my work in elections is the most meaningful because it is the clearest example of why the lack of consistent investment in technology has failed to help people exercise their rights as citizens and is contributing to the further erosion of faith in our democratic process.

Prior to 2008, I did not give much thought to the operational side of elections. My focus was on get-out-the-vote and voter education efforts from the political side. I took for granted the relative ease of my personal experience: going to my local polling place, being a fluent English speaker, and having no accessibility needs.

My perspective shifted dramatically with the introduction of direct-recording electronic (DRE) voting machines in my county. I saw the promise of DREs to make it easier for some voters while also recognizing that the move away from handwritten ballots would be a challenge for other voters as well as poll workers. I immediately signed up to be a poll worker and spent the next several years leveraging my comfort with technology to help both groups. The lessons that I learned being behind the scenes on election nights were critical in informing my approach to the hows and whys of rolling out new election technology to meet the needs of voters and election administrators.

According to the Census Bureau, voter participation in U.S. elections is roughly half of our 255 million citizens of voting age. This gap exists despite the tremendous efforts by election officials, community groups, and national organizations to raise awareness, interest, and participation in voting. Politics and political identity have become a larger part of everyday life for many Americans, resulting in greater polarization and lower trust in democratic processes. People are becoming increasingly skeptical of every step of the electoral process. Yet for the other half of the eligible population that declined to vote, the most common answer given for not voting was "too busy, conflicting work or school schedule." Solving for that pain point should be the focus of election administrators, technology providers, and other stakeholders. The question that they should all be asking is: "What is needed to scale today's election infrastructure to meet the needs of voters if participation increased by 20 percent, 30 percent, 40 percent, or even 50 percent in the next generation?"

I believe that the only way to serve current and future voters is the introduction of more, not less, digital technology to address usability and risks in the categories of accountability, accessibility, and security. The baseline for evaluating integration of new technologies should be a comparison against the current implementation of the system as a whole rather than theoretical perfection of a single component. In addition, there must be a frank recognition that never in the history of democracies has all risk been eliminated from elections. We all accept some risk in a variety of complex systems in our daily lives, because we understand that completely eliminating risks is often too expensive and infeasible. Adding complexity—including people, processes, and technologies—to electoral systems has in fact been necessary to accommodate the growth in the number of eligible voters resulting from the expansion of voting rights to citizens based on age, gender, race, and property ownership. Digital technology specifically has been necessary to meet the legal requirements based on a voter's location, language, and accessibility needs. Lastly, digital technologies have enabled improvements in resiliency and accountability in times of conflict, disaster, and other community emergencies.

My vision for the future of voting is a flexible system that places in-person, by-mail, and digital participation options on an equal level of trustworthiness in the minds of voters. Voters should only have to be concerned with their personal preferences and convenience when deciding how to cast their ballot. Election administrators should have the freedom to craft tailored experiences in virtual spaces when physical space or personnel are not available or not feasible. This vision fundamentally requires a strong commitment

to solving the challenges of trustworthiness and auditability underlying mobile voting solutions. Those challenges are not insur-
mountable. However, adequately addressing them starts with the
belief that it is possible and worth doing. That is what I choose to
believe. The next step is inspiring engineers, investors, researchers,
policymakers, and other stakeholders to work together toward the
goal of making voting more accountable, accessible, and secure for
today's voters and the more than 120 million citizens who are eligible but choose not to vote.

AVALON ZBOROVSKY-FENSTER

· *Student Scholar, Institute of Global Politics, Columbia University*

The first time I voted in an election as a newly registered eighteen-year-old in 2020, I learned about how to do it on my phone. I messaged an automated texting line to find out where my polling place was. I used digital news to educate myself on the various ballot propositions that were up for a vote. I learned about candidates through their websites and stayed updated on election results through social media. It was seamless.

The only part of the process I didn't do on my phone was the act of voting itself. I stepped away from my schoolwork for the day, had my parents drive me to my polling place, and stood on line for about an hour and a half before I was able to cast my vote. It felt odd that so much of my political world was happening digitally, but this one aspect of the process remained unchanged. I knew countless students and would-be first-time voters who were also in college, but since the process of getting an absentee ballot was wrought with so many obstacles, and they couldn't afford to physically travel home just for election day, they just didn't vote. A shame.

In high school, I was considered a youth activist—one of those young people that older organizers and politicians would call on when they needed passion and momentum brought to their protest or campaign. I was working for March for Our Lives on national organizing and social media and traveled across the country to meet other youth activists, presidential candidates, and history-making political thinkers who offered to support our work. However, no matter how far I traveled from my hometown on Long Island, I was greeted with the already familiar faces of other young people, because we were all already so connected digitally. We often reposted each other's initiatives and calls-to-action on social media to get the word out to more students around America, and we spent countless hours on video calls strategizing about how to counter the political polarization that was being exacerbated by our leaders. None of this digital interaction in our change-making work felt difficult. It felt natural, because we were raised on it. And no matter how much the "grown-ups" would poke fun at our tech usage, the truth was we were mobilizing initially disengaged students at levels that no one could truly demean, and we did it by meeting them where they were at: on their phones.

Fast-forward a few years ahead, I'm now twenty-one years old and majoring in political science and human rights and minoring in science, public policy, and ethics at Barnard College of Columbia University. To be honest, it was my initial real-world experiences in activism—where I watched how tech can activate people's hearts and minds to drive positive change—that made clear to me the profound potential of technology to reshape our political landscape. In response, I've worked in both houses of Congress, with several Fortune 50 tech companies on federal and global policy on issues like artificial intelligence, human rights, and the digital divide, and for many national nonprofits focusing on justice and the law.

I'm a student scholar at the Columbia Institute of Global Politics, focusing on the intersection of technological innovation and political change. I even started my own platform that uses social media and other digital technologies to educate hundreds of thousands of young women around the world on how to break through the "glass floor" of their early career. Through all of these experiences, I've witnessed firsthand the remarkable ease with which Gen Z and Gen Alpha navigate the digital world and innately understand its challenges and benefits. And it seems that while we've got it pretty figured out, older generations are still debating whether or not phones can be a valuable tool for more than entertainment. (Spoiler: of course they can.)

Let me make myself explicitly clear: my peers and I are more than mere consumers of technology; we are its architects, advocates, and pioneers. Our comfort and proficiency in handling complex online platforms, leveraging the power of social media, and harnessing technology to amplify our voices is unparalleled. We understand it like one understands their first language, and it's unfortunate that this truth is often shirked by our leaders as frivolous rather than embraced.

In a democracy, the system is entirely reliant on our participation to make it continue to function as intended. When someone experiences barriers to voting—a fundamental piece of the process—not only are they inhibited from doing their civic duty, but they also get the message that their vote isn't important enough for our leaders to make it easier for them. For young people, feeling this way as first-time voters does nothing to inspire them to become civically engaged in the long term. For my friends who couldn't get access to an absentee ballot in the 2020 election, their fears about our system seemed to be confirmed: there's too much bureaucracy for things to ever change, no one cares about my vote or voice, and one can't trust our leaders to make things effective, so what's the point? In a time where there is so much dysfunction, polarization, and vicious partisanship, the last thing our leaders should be doing is perpetuating apathy among our rising citizenry.

When I learned about the concept of mobile voting, in my eyes, it aligned seamlessly with our digital-native identity. It represents a natural progression, allowing us to leverage our fluency to enhance the democratic process—something our generations care deeply about. By having the ability to securely cast a vote on our phone, the process can become far more intuitive and accessible to generations who have so much to lose by not electing leaders that truly care about the problems that impact us. And instead of just writing it off as impractical or too forward-thinking, leaders across the aisle—many of whom claim they care about advancing the United States as an unparalleled leaders in civics—ought to let go of myopic thinking and embrace new tools that can help us move the needle forward on issues that are only becoming more urgent. Virtue signaling in conversations about technology's use in our democracy is wholly unproductive, and we actually make it harder to manage potential risks by taking an entirely cynical approach on the value of these tools in our democracy.

We are in a state of emergency. While older generations can recall achieving lifelong goals at my age, I'm wary of determining

my goals five years in advance since I feel so much uncertain-
ty about what the future looks like. I know from countless conversations with peers that I am not alone in this. While there are
always ebbs and flows in American politics, we have too many fires
burning, too little time to put all of them out, and too few leaders
that are willing to change their old ways in our new times. Our
democracy needs to find and test long-term solutions, like mobile
voting—not just Band-Aid approaches that are informed by the
way the world worked decades ago. In the history of humanity, we
have always needed to adapt in order to survive and carry on. What
are we waiting for now?

FRANCISCO AGUILAR

· *Nevada Secretary of State*

As Nevada's newest secretary of state, I get to take pride every day in the work of elections officials across the state. The team in my office, and teams in offices in every county and large city in Nevada, labor tirelessly (election year or not) to run some of the country's most secure and accessible elections. Every active registered voter gets a ballot in the mail, there are generous early voting periods, and voters can register to vote up until the close of polls. Certain voters in Nevada also have access to a form of mobile voting—but before I get into the details of that technology, I want to briefly talk about why accessible elections are so important to me.

Before I became elected, I spent decades of my life working in education. It taught me about what's important to kids and young adults and how to get them engaged and excited about their schooling, jobs, and community. As part of that work, I founded a workforce-focused college preparatory high school in one of North Las Vegas's most vulnerable communities. The student body is 85 percent Latino and 10 percent Black. Before the 2020 presidential election, I talked to these kids and asked them if their parents were planning to vote. They told me no. They told me their vote doesn't matter, and people don't care what they think.

I decided to run for secretary of state because I knew this mindset had to change. Our vulnerable and historically marginalized communities can and have the ability to decide crucial elections—and their voices are some of the most important. But if we want them to participate in our democracy, we have to meet them where they're at.

In Nevada, we've seen in the span of just two years how much accessibility can impact voter turnout. In 2020, during the height of the COVID-19 pandemic, the secretary of state, in coordination with the seventeen county election officials, approved a plan to send registered voters a mail ballot. This was done out of an abundance of caution for voters, election officials, and poll workers alike. Lawmakers followed suit by calling a special legislative session later that year and in 2021 made Nevada a permanent vote-by-mail state—making us one of only eight states that allow all elections to be conducted by mail, alongside California, Colorado, Hawaii, Oregon, Utah, Vermont, and Washington. Historic use of mail ballots, or absentee ballots as they were called back then, typically hovered around 6 percent of the method of voting during a presidential general election and as low as 2 percent during a midterm primary election. Since then, the percentage has rapidly increased, with over half of the ballots cast in the 2022 general election being by mail.

While this originally was created to curb the spread of COVID-19 during a critical presidential election, the positive impacts have gone far beyond that.

Thanks to the work of tribal governments and Nevada's county clerks, this increased access saw turnout in Native communities jump by 25 percent in the 2020 election. Before the passage of universal mail ballots, tribal voters were often forced to travel hundreds of miles to vote. In Nevada, this could mean driving through snow, rain, or windstorms during the general election period. Understanding democracy, researching who you're voting for and what ballot questions mean is already hard enough; this additional barrier was blocking out an entire community.

Nevada's leaders have taken some of the most significant steps in the country to expand access to voting. But in an age where you can order a pizza from your phone and track the pizza from the second your order is received to the time it's on your doorstep, people want to know why they don't have that same level of accessibility and information in every aspect of their lives. Government has adapted to the online world in some ways, like allowing you to pay certain fees or taxes or register to vote. Government should also explore ways to extend that access to the full voting experience, meeting the digital generation where they're at.

By 2024, Millennials and Gen Z will make up 40 percent of the electorate and become the largest voting bloc. The kids at the school I founded clearly become more empowered when they're given the authority to take charge of their own lives. That means giving them the tools they need to succeed and make a difference; voting can be that key. Every issue they care about goes through the ballot box. When you give young adults, like the ones at my school, the tools and information they need to get out and vote, they have the power to create generational change for their families. We just need to figure out the right technological innovation to meet them where they're at.

Now I want to talk about one of Nevada's most important accessibility tools—one that allows our citizens to vote by phone and one we could use to expand that access. Nevada's Effective Absentee System for Elections (which we call EASE) is an online application that integrates voter registration and offers a method of electronic ballot delivery (among several methods). This was created for military and overseas voters but has since been expanded by legislative action to provide access to disabled voters and tribal voters.

There are several important security checks and balances to EASE. If you use it to cast your ballot online, with your cell phone for example, the ballot is transmitted to the county via secure file transfer protocol (FTP) connection. The county then creates a printed duplicate of the ballot and puts it through the same process as other physical ballots to ensure that there is no risk of fraud or duplication. This combination of physical and cybersecurity is vital to our process, and it could potentially be difficult to scale to an entire nation. But the EASE system represents the kind of success we can have when government focuses on innovation and problem-solving, and I've made a pledge to expand it as much as possible.

Accessibility doesn't have to come at the expense of election security. The Nevada Secretary of State's Office continuously assesses and works to improve cybersecurity across all of our divisions, but especially as it relates to elections. While our IT staff continues to go through high-level cybersecurity training, our elections staff is collaborating with federal, state, and county partners to ensure safeguards are in place for data sharing. This team does great work to audit vulnerabilities and strengths within these systems. There is always room for improvement in security, and there will always be threats, as we are a high-level office with a lot of eyes on us, no matter what method of voting is used. We can mitigate cyber threats at the same time we work on increasing access to the ballot box. You can send millions of dollars online through a wire transfer. Once the public government is ready for it, the technology for secure electronic voting is there to keep it secure.

We know the world is moving in this direction already, and we know what the next generation will expect. As elected officials, we need to develop a strategy to take the next steps to increase participation in our democracy, improve election security, and make voting more convenient. And if we're being honest with ourselves, no strategy makes sense if it doesn't include the concept of mobile voting. We just need to figure out how to make it happen; I'm proud Nevada will be on the front lines.

KATHERINE GEHL

· *Former CEO of Gehl Foods*
· *Originator of final five voting*
· *Founder and chairman of the Institute*
for Political Innovation

Everything I need to know about politics I learned from cheese. In the last decade of my business career, I ran a $250 million food company in Wisconsin. We sold cheese— cheese sauce, actually—in stadiums and theaters around the country. If people liked my cheese, I did well. If they didn't, they bought cheese from someone else. That's healthy competition. Healthy competition propels businesses to make better products. Better products equal happier customers. And happy customers equal successful businesses. Win-win. Now, while I was running Gehl Foods, I was also deeply involved in—and increasingly frustrated with—politics. The more frustrated I got, the more I wondered why politics wasn't more like cheese.

Why do both parties—the Democrats and the Republicans— keep doing so well when their customers (that's us!) are so unhappy? Why is the politics industry win-lose? They win. We lose. The reason? It turns out that the only thing almost all Americans agree on—Washington is broken—is also the one thing we're all wrong about. The truth is Washington isn't broken; it's doing exactly what it's designed to do. Americans from coast to coast wrongly believe the system was designed to serve us, the voters, the citizens, the public interest. The truth is that most of the rules in politics are set by and for the benefit of our two political parties and their surrounding companies in the politics business. And they're all doing great—even as the American public has never been more dissatisfied. Said another way: politics isn't broken…it's fixed.

This is a guiding principle of politics industry theory, the nonpartisan body of work I originated and championed. To be clear: I don't believe our problems are caused by the Republicans or the Democrats, or the existence of parties, or even having just two major parties. The problem is that under the current rules, the current two are guaranteed to remain the only two, regardless of what they do or don't get done on behalf of our country. And senators and representatives are prisoners of the system also. Their only option is lockstep allegiance to their side. So, what do we do about it? How do we change the game to make politics win-win? By changing the rules. But which ones? There are hundreds of bad rules in politics, but by looking at the system through a competition lens, we can identify the two rules—not gerrymandering, not campaign finance, not term limits—that are both our biggest obstacles and our biggest opportunities.

Bad Rule #1: Party Primaries

You all know primaries, those first-round elections that we mostly ignore. The ones that determine the single Republican and the single Democrat who can appear on the November general election ballot. Party primaries have become low-turnout elections dominated by highly ideological voters, special interests, and donors. Candidates know that the only way to make it to the general election is to win the favor of these more extreme partisans in the primary. So, candidates from both parties have little choice but to move toward the extremes. Why does this matter? Because it dramatically affects governing—and not in a good way.

Imagine you're a member of Congress. You're deciding whether to pass a bill that addresses a critical national challenge. You might ask yourself: "Is this a good idea? Is this what the majority of my constituents want?" But that's not how it works. The question that matters most to you is: "Will I win my next party primary if I vote for this?" And the answer is almost always no. Compromise solutions don't win party primaries. There is virtually no intersection between Congress acting in the public interest and the likelihood of its members getting reelected. In other words, If America's elected representatives do their jobs the way we need them to, they're likely to lose their jobs. That's crazy. No wonder Washington doesn't get anything done.

Bad Rule #2: Plurality Voting

In any other industry as big and thriving as politics, with this much customer dissatisfaction and only two rivals, some entrepreneur would see a phenomenal business opportunity and create a new competitor responding to what customers want. But that doesn't happen in politics because of one big rule that keeps out almost all new competition: plurality voting. It sounds fancy, but it simply means the candidate with the most votes wins. Seems logical, but it's actually a huge mistake. Why? Because in the United States, you can win an election *even* if the majority of voters didn't vote for you. Thanks to plurality voting, we may not vote for the candidate we really want because we're afraid we will waste our vote or, even worse, we'll spoil the election.

The spoiler and wasted-vote problems are the single biggest reason almost nobody new ever runs. And if there's never any new competition, the existing parties aren't accountable to us for results because they don't need us to like what they're doing. They only need us to choose them as the lesser of two evils. Does this sound like the best we can do—in America? It doesn't have to be this way.

The election innovation we need is final five voting. The name itself sounds like a healthy competition. Here's how it works. First, we eliminate closed, party-controlled primaries. We replace them with open, nonpartisan primaries where the top five finishers advance to the November general election. Then, in the general election, we eliminate plurality voting and use instant runoffs to elect the candidate with the greatest appeal to the greatest number of voters—and to eliminate the spoiler problem we just talked about. Because we use an *open* primary, all the candidates are on the same ballot regardless of party. When the results are tallied, the five most popular candidates—again, regardless of party—move on to the general election. In the general election, voters rank this "final five" from most favorite to least favorite.

Final five voting gives voters more choice, more voice, and better results because it transforms the incentives in politics. Now, the message to Congress is do your job or lose your job. Innovate, reach across the aisle if you need to, come up with real solutions to our problems, and create new opportunities for progress—or be guaranteed healthy competition in the next election. It's the best of what I call free market politics: innovation, results, and account-ability. Just imagine what we could do with that!

Not only is final five voting a powerful innovation, but it is achievable (in years, not decades!). As of this writing in the fall of 2023, Alaska has passed and already successfully used a variation of final five voting with great success. We have a number of states on target for ballot initiatives in 2024, as well as a very strong pipeline of states for 2026. The most up-to-date information can be found on the national campaign website, finalfivevoting.org.

It's exciting to think about final five voting paired with mobile voting. Mobile voting will make voting easier and more accessible, while final five voting will ensure that votes in the general election actually matter. The two, used in concert, could produce powerful results and move us closer to our vision of a more effective, more representative legislature.

ROB RICHIE

· *Cofounder of FairVote in 1992, CEO until 2023*
· *Advisor to FairVote & other electoral
reform organizations*

t's time to rank the vote. To reverse our republic's downward spiral, we must stop limiting voters to a single preference in elections that under our traditional voting rules self-destruct with more than two candidates.

However tempting, blaming our politicians for our current failures isn't enough. Rules always matter, and our voting rules have constantly evolved as each new generation of politicians learns how to make existing rules work for their partisan goals.

American democracy is most threatened when we allow our rules to become static. In our ongoing quest to achieve a more perfect union, who votes and how we vote have regularly changed—and despite disturbing regressions along the way, usually for the better. That results in an ongoing dance between politicians seeking to serve their interests and democracy champions seeking a more perfect union. That sometimes puts them fiercely at odds, but at other times working together to expand suffrage to more Americans, directly elect more offices, modernize election administration, and improve tools to be informed voters.

No single reform is ever enough on its own. But ranked-choice voting is eminently winnable across our states—and nicely complements other changes like bringing more voters in and providing simple ballot interfaces with mobile voting, erasing the gerrymandered lines that strangle voter choice, and ensuring voters have access to more accurate information about their choices.

ranked-choice voting has become the nation's fastest-growing electoral reform for good reasons. It's improving the biggest elections in Alaska, Maine, and more than fifty local governments, from New York City to conservative towns in suburban Utah. Longer term, it has time on its side: young Americans typically approve ranked-choice voting by margins of three-to-one in ballot measures and have enacted it for student government elections at some 100 colleges and universities.

What explains RCV's appeal? Voters are hungry to be free to express what they think. We seek elections that bring representatives closer to the people. We want elected leaders to hear our voices and collectively capture our nuanced views that fill out the growing gaps in representation that have sent American democracy into a "doom loop" of binary action and reaction that threatens our deepest values. We want to hold elected leaders accountable for delivering on the promise of timely policy and effective governance.

Through the simple change of allowing voters to rank candidates in order of preference—starting with a first choice and continuing with an optional second choice, third choice, and so on—ranked-choice voting is a linchpin toward achieving better elections.

Your ballot becomes a straightforward tool to ensure your voice is heard. Your vote initially counts only for your first choice—just as now. But suppose your first choice loses due to being in last place. Rather than your vote being set aside and not affecting the outcome among the remaining candidates, you've already shared how you want your vote to count in the second: for the candidate ranked next on your ballot choice. After three rounds of counting, the three weakest candidates in a five-candidate race would be eliminated. The contest then becomes an "instant runoff" between the two strongest candidates where all voters have had a chance with their ranking to indicate their choice between them without having to return to the polls.

Ranked-choice voting means a lot more votes to count—underscoring its appeal to any group concerned about voter turnout and voting rights. No more primaries won with a quarter of the vote over the opposition of 75 percent of voters. No more delayed, expensive, and deeply negative runoffs. No more "spoilers" and shaming of third-party and independent candidates—rather, we can have an entirely new choice to the same tired old candidates who would never run in today's rules. With ranked-choice voting, we can have majority rule while giving everyone a better chance to be heard and rewarding candidates for building bridges rather than destroying them.

Ranked-choice voting is a proven system dating back more than 150 years. Australia and Ireland have elected their top leaders with it for more than a century, and countless private organizations use it at the recommendation of parliamentary guides like *Robert's Rules of Order*.

Ranked-choice voting's reform moment has come in the United States. As shown in dozens of cities, it's more efficient and less costly than traditional runoff elections that have become harder to run well with today's expensive elections and campaign finance system run amok. It's more representative than plurality voting rules that allow majorities to split their vote and elect leaders who aren't even trying to represent most Americans.

Sick of primary elections with crowded fields that generate weak and unrepresentative nominees? Then turn to ranked-choice voting. Find it ridiculous that a 49 percent to 48 percent result in Georgia will trigger statewide runoffs—ones coming with hundreds of millions of dollars in new ads and taxpayers having to shoulder $75 million in costs—to find out who was the second choice of the handful of voters who backed the Libertarian candidate? Ranked-choice voting is your answer; it is already used by all overseas military voters in Georgia who today return a ranked-choice ballot to count in any race that might go to a runoff.

Do you wish politicians spent less time attacking their opponents? Ranked-choice voting rewards candidates who find connections with their opponents, promoting more civility on the campaign trail and often electing candidates who have earned a positive ranking from more than two-thirds of voters.

What makes its expansion so urgent is that it offers a deeply American response to our nation's unique challenges—ones tied to our nation's unique combination of constitutional structures and political traditions. Given the destructive but effective tactics of our twenty-first-century politicians, we need ranked-choice voting up and down our ballots because we urgently need more than two choices on our ballots across all fifty states.

Fundamentally, binary politics is broken. Those who think that limiting Americans to the same two parties is fundamental to our republic are unaware of how our party system in the nineteenth century regularly evolved—and they are blind to the underlying reasons for our accelerating slide into an era of deeply polarized parties who whip up their party bases through hatred and fear of the other party.

It doesn't have to be this way. Australia has had ranked-choice voting for a century, and seven candidates on average run for every seat. The two biggest parties usually win, but they always face competition, and their candidates always have to reach out to backers of independents and emerging parties to compete for their backup preferences. And they'll lose when they refuse to adapt—as the "teal independents" showed in 2022 when defeating a string of incumbents who refused to adapt to greater voter interest in tackling political corruption, gender equality, and climate change. Given disenchantment with the major parties and their deepening polarization, it's only a matter of time before more Americans turn to new parties and independents. Shaming potential new parties will stop working. Before that happens, we'll want to build on ranked-choice voting's progress to accommodate greater voter choice.

Looking to ranked-choice voting over time, it's particularly impactful when twinned with multimember districts—as proposed in the Fair Representation Act in Congress that by statute can "save

American democracy," in the words of *New York Times* columnist David Brooks. It would effectively end gerrymandering, give every voter a meaningful choice in every election, open representation for both major parties in every district, and provide a direct solution to binary polarization and how best to sustain a multiracial democracy that brings in more women, people of color, and people with different views into Congress, state legislatures, and local elections.

As I look back on my three decades of increasingly impactful advocacy for ranked-choice voting, I would say that the single biggest barrier to progress has been our antiquated election administration regime—one tied to limited funding, private voting equipment companies that struggle to turn profits, and cautious election administrators who focus more on delivering basic services than on innovation. Fortunately, we're gradually removing those barriers so that we can have transparent, fast, effective, secure, and affordable ranked-choice-voting elections anywhere they're passed.

As mobile voting addresses security concerns and gains a foothold, it's a particularly strong fit for the ranked-choice-voting ballot—as already demonstrated by many colleges and organizations. The mobile voting interface makes it easy for voters to rank their ballots without error and to show results that are intuitive and clear. Elections that combine these changes would liberate voters to more fully realize the promise of government of, by, and for the people.

MARK A. RICCOBONO

· *President, National Federation of the Blind*

t was a pleasantly cool evening in Madison, Wisconsin, on that
November Tuesday in 1996 when I went to vote in a presidential election for the first time. I was thrilled to exercise this
important right and responsibility. I had no real concept of what
my rights were as a voter in America beyond my study of the revolution that established our democracy. I certainly knew nothing
about my rights as a blind voter in America. I had been to the polls
during many elections with my parents, who are not blind, but gave
no thought to the process or how it might be different for me as a
person who could not read or mark the standard ballot by myself. I
believed that the only option I would have to fulfill my right to vote
would be to trust some unknown poll worker to mark my ballot as
I directed. The thrill of that first voting experience quickly wore off
as the delightful older woman who assisted me repeated my choices
back to me in a loud voice. Whether her volume had to do with
her own inability to hear or her misunderstanding that she had to
speak louder for a blind person to hear her, I will never know. I do

know that it was the beginning of my realization that there is more to voting than simply the power of placing the ballot into the box at the end of the process.

The National Federation of the Blind, America's transformative membership organization of blind people, was established in 1940 and has been essential to raising the expectations for blind voters to have a private and independently markable ballot. Years after my first voting experience, I learned that there was a time when blind people did not even have a choice about who assisted them at the polls. In many places, an official from each party would stand with the blind person while the ballot was marked. I learned that because of the advocacy work of the federation, the laws were changed so that blind people could choose who assisted them at the polls. When I moved to Maryland in 2003, I learned that blind people in that state had fought for a tactile ballot system that allowed blind people to independently mark their choices—although those selections would later need to be transcribed to a standard ballot. While this approach did provide more independence and arguably more privacy, it still left an element of trust and potential human error (or dishonest transcription)—a risk other voters did not face. Many other states and municipalities had attempted to develop similar ballot-marking methods for blind people, but, like Maryland, each approach fell short of equaling the privacy and independence of the average American voter. In 2002, the passage of the Help America Vote Act (HAVA) presented a transformative opportunity to eliminate the barriers to privacy and accessibility in the voting process.

Due to the advocacy work of the federation, specific language was included in HAVA to provide for nonvisual access to voting systems. The bill required that at least one accessible voting machine be available in all polling places for federal elections. This meant that, at least in federal elections, blind people might have a private and independent voting experience. I can still clearly remember my first experience going to the polls to vote on a fully accessible, electronic ballot-marking device—being able to read the ballot, mark my choices independently, and review my selections without anyone else knowing how I voted; it was a powerful experience.

Yet within a decade after the implementation of HAVA, many states were moving away from voting machines due to security concerns. The result has been that electronic ballot-marking devices are treated as a second-class option, and blind voters encounter accessibility and privacy barriers.

Once we, as blind people, experienced the true power of voting privately and independently, we determined never to be shut out again. We have continued to press for the implementation of fully accessible ballot-marking devices and to protect the standard established through HAVA. Beyond HAVA, we have successfully advocated that the Americans with Disabilities Act (ADA) applies in voting discrimination cases. Regulations issued under Title II of the ADA require state and local boards of elections to provide appropriate auxiliary aids and services to provide voters with disabilities an equal opportunity to participate in, and enjoy the benefits of, programs and services offered in a manner that protects the privacy and independence of voters with disabilities.

Beyond the law, the lived experience of blind people has taught us that there are irrational barriers built into election systems. For blind Americans, the experience of voting is not a joyous opportunity to participate in our democracy but rather a test of overcoming adversity. In addition to the accessibility barriers that blind people face in all forms of voting even today, data gathered by the federation in elections going back to 2008 demonstrate that blind people continue to encounter demoralizing treatment and receive misinformation about their rights from poll workers who have not been properly trained. Advocacy, poll-worker training, monitoring of boards of elections, and voter education are all activities the federation continues to pursue daily. However, our energy and resources would be better invested in a future where voting is more private, more independent, and dramatically free of the existing barriers.

In 2012, we established a mobile voting working group to explore new options for providing greater access to voting for all, and to educate the thought leaders on the key elements needed to build in equal access for the blind. We believe that America has the innovative capacity to fulfill its promise of being a democracy of the people, for the people. The same nation that can put people in orbit, engineer rapid medical responses to a worldwide pandemic, and generate the most cutting-edge technologies on the planet can certainly develop an accessible, secure, and reliable set of tools to empower all Americans to vote privately and independently.

All three of my daughters will be reaching voting age by 2030. Each of them, for various reasons, might face barriers in accessing their right to vote. All of these barriers are artificial and removable by making a commitment to innovating a solution that provides privacy, independence, and access to as many people as possible. Our nation has the capacity and passionate advocates like those in the

National Federation of the Blind who are ready to help. The only remaining question is whether we can bring together a community big enough to make the promise a reality. It's people like me, an average blind person who goes to vote in every election despite the barriers I know I will encounter, who have the most at stake by not working toward this future. It is not elected leaders; we are the ones who have the most to lose—the everyday Americans who seek to live in a nation that reflects our hopes and dreams. When our voice is more fully incorporated into the American democracy we will experience the power and wisdom of the people as envisioned by the crafters of our nation. I am prepared to work toward that future and eliminate those barriers—are you prepared to work with me?

PART 5

WHAT YOU CAN DO ABOUT IT

CHAPTER 10

....

GEN Z AND GEN ALPHA
ARE THE FUTURE NOW

n law school, I took a class from a professor named Abner Mikva. Mikva had been a federal judge, served as White House counsel, served in Congress, and had a generally incredible career. By the time I got to him, he was nearing the end of his career, and his class was mainly him just telling stories from his life. I loved it. His story about his first day in politics explains the situation well.

As I remember it, Mikva grew up in Chicago and decided he wanted to get involved in politics. So he went to the office of the local ward committeeman—a guy by the name of Tim O'Sullivan—and said he wanted to work on Adlai Stevenson's 1948 gubernatorial campaign.

"Who sent you?" O'Sullivan asked Mikva.

"Nobody," Mikva replied.

O'Sullivan takes a long drag on his cigar, looked Mikva in the eye, and said, "We don't want nobody that nobody sent."

Seventy-five years later, the style of politics has changed a lot, but the substance? Not so much. Fresh faces are suspicious. New ideas are dangerous. It's all about risk aversion.

The people in power on both sides of the aisle will come up with every excuse they can to avoid implementing mobile voting—because they know exactly what it means. It means you'll vote in much greater numbers. You'll hold them accountable for actual progress and actual results. And if they don't deliver, you'll throw them out. That scares the shit out of them.*

Now, before you say to yourself, "Fine, but I'm still just one person; what difference can I really make?" think about the power you, as a generation, have. There are an estimated 70 million members of Gen Z and another estimated 51 million of Gen Alpha (as of 2022).[1] By 2028, these groups will be the largest group of eligible voters in the country. By 2034, you will be the largest generation ever. And you are the first digitally native generation. You intuitively understand the role of technology in day-to-day life in a way your parents and grandparents never could. Just look at the statistics:

- The average Gen Zer or Gen Alpha gets a mobile phone at age twelve with adoption expected to reach 96.9 percent by 2026.[2]

- More than three-quarters of Gen Z, defined as those born between 1996 and 2010, claim to have gotten their first

---

* That's why states like Texas and Georgia in recent years have passed legislation attempting to significantly restrict access to the ballot box, even beyond its already sizable limitations. It's why ideas like paper ballots only are so crazy. In a world that's literally burning, in a world where we desperately need action by our leaders, the paper ballot advocates would rather take us back in time and see even fewer people vote.

smartphone before the age of eighteen, compared to only 49 percent of millennials.[3]

- Nearly 9 in 10 U.S. Gen Z adults spend more than an hour on social media each day, and nearly half spend more than three hours with the platforms.[4]

- According to a Statista report on internet users, there were 307.34 million internet users in the United States in 2022 (out of a total population of 333 million, so 92 percent). Of those, 282.48 million have mobile devices, so approximately 85 percent of the U.S. population has a smartphone or tablet.[†] The United States has the third-largest digital population in the world, after China and India. Ninety-seven percent of adults aged eighteen to twenty-nine reported owning a smartphone in 2022. As of December 2022, eighteen- to twenty-nine-year-olds are the most active internet users. "Nearly half of them stated being almost constantly online."[5]

- A 2022 Pew Research study about teens, social media, and tech found that 95 percent of teens now say they have or have access to a smartphone. Ninety percent of teens have access to a desktop or laptop computer at home, and 97 percent of teens use the internet daily.[6]

---

† Keep in mind, we're not arguing to replace existing forms of voting with mobile voting. Physical ballot boxes should stay. So should mail-in voting. This is just giving people another way to participate, and more than 85 percent of them already own the technology needed to do so.

Because much of your political life has been dominated by the Trump era, you also intuitively understand how bad things are and how badly change is needed. And if you're taking the time to read this book, the problem isn't that you don't care. Apathy isn't the reason for low turnout. It's that we deliberately foster a system of voting designed to keep you away. Because as long as you don't show up, you don't matter. And as long as you don't matter, politicians can go about their day without worrying about what you think or what you want.

Your participation in the process *by not voting* is exactly what they want. Or as Arndrea Waters King, president of the Drum Major Institute, said so perfectly at our SXSW panel: "If you don't think that your right to vote is powerful, then why are they trying so hard to take that right away from you?"

But how do we know Gen Z can produce real change? Because it's already happening.

THE FIRST GEN Z MEMBER OF CONGRESS

Maxwell Frost was fifteen when the Sandy Hook school shooting occurred in Connecticut, taking twenty-six lives, including those of twenty children. Frost lived in Orlando and decided he needed to do something about the ever-increasing flow of guns and shootings. He even flew to Connecticut to figure out how he could help. He started working as a national organizer for March for Our Lives, a group created by high school students in the wake of the Parkland school shooting.

A decade later, shootings in schools, churches, and Walmarts have continued unabated. Frost realized that in the case of guns, you need federal legislation to do anything meaningful. Individual states can and do ban certain types of guns, but there is no way to stop guns from crossing state lines, leaving us all at the mercy of the states with the fewest restrictions. Truly impactful reform can only come from the federal level.

Frost looked at the dysfunction that gripped Congress and knew that expecting them to get it done on their own would never happen. Could one new member of Congress really make a difference? Maybe. He decided to try.

In 2022, Frost launched a bid for the House of Representatives. His odds of winning were low. Really low—he was facing not one, but two former members of Congress in the primary, Corrine Brown and Alan Grayson. How'd he do it? By leaning into what should have been his biggest weakness—his age and lack of experience.

Frost ran on a message of generational change, out with the old, in with the new. He focused on gun violence of course, but also Medicare for All and canceling student debt. He raised more money online than any other candidate. He scored endorsements from Senators Bernie Sanders and Elizabeth Warren. He dominated media coverage, dominated social media, and developed an effective grassroots operation. He won the primary—and then cruised to victory in the general election because, thanks to gerrymandering, there were barely any Republicans in his district.

It wasn't easy. Unlike most candidates for office, Frost didn't have any money to fuel his campaign. He didn't even have enough money to pay the rent, so he started driving for Uber between campaign events (seriously).[7] He couch surfed, even staying with his sister's ex-boyfriend for a while. Frost was sworn into office at the age of twenty-six. The average age in the House of Representatives was fifty-eight (which is youthful compared to the Senate, where the average age is sixty-five).[8] No one in the establishment wanted Maxwell Frost to win. But he did. And he proved we can too.

The Parkland shooting brought Maxwell Frost to the forefront of political activism, but what makes Frost interesting isn't that he's a complete outlier. It's that he's an indication of something much bigger. (It feels almost trite to tell the story of Greta Thunberg since everyone already knows that one, but she's another example of how someone in Gen Z was able to use technology and media to help spark a global movement.)

Gen Z Activism around School Shootings

Tufts University's Center for Information & Research on Civic Learning and Engagement studied the influence of the gun-violence prevention movement on youth turnout in the 2018 election.[9] They found that two-thirds of youths (meaning people ages eighteen to twenty-four) said they had paid either some or a lot of attention to the Parkland shooting. The study also found that young people who agreed with the post-Parkland movement were 21 percent more likely to have voted that year.

Keep in mind, this was back in 2018. The internet wasn't what it is today. Shootings have only gotten worse. And every kid in virtually every school lives with school shootings not just as a concept but as a reality via active shooter drills. So awareness of this issue has risen significantly even since 2018.

In fact, after a school shooting in Nashville in April 2023, thousands of Tennessee students walked out of class to march on the state capitol to demand that politicians start protecting them. Pre-internet, the rest of the world would have learned about this on that evening's news or in the next day's newspaper. But instead, thanks to all of the different social platforms, kids all over the country knew about the protest before it even happened. And they joined in. My daughter and her friends walked out of their school in protest—almost 1,000 miles away in New York City—as did kids everywhere. Think about what that meant for the impact of the original organizers in Nashville. They were able to spark protests nationwide.

The impact Gen Z can have on policy isn't just limited to government. Fox News host Laura Ingraham spent an inordinate amount of time ridiculing Parkland survivor and gun safety activist David Hogg on her show. Hogg, who wrote the foreword of this book, accused her of cyberbullying and called on her show's sponsors to cancel their advertising buys. Hogg's followers ran with it—and succeeded.

Here's the list of companies that canceled their advertising on Ingraham's show—Ace Hardware, Allstate, Arby's, AT&T, Atlantis Paradise Island, Bayer, Blue Apron, Entertainment Studios, Expedia, Honda, Hulu, IBM, Jenny Craig, Johnson & Johnson, JoS A. Bank, Liberty Mutual, Miracle-Ear, Mitsubishi Motors, Nestlé, Nutrish, Office Depot, Principal Financial Group, Rocket Mortgage, Ruby Tuesday, Sleep Number, SlimFast, Stitch Fix, TripAdvisor, and Wayfair. Ingraham was forced to publicly apologize to Hogg and there's no doubt that other media personalities took notice.[10]*

---

* Hogg then went on to found a new political action committee called Leaders We Deserve that backs candidates under thirty-five years old running for federal office and under thirty years old running for state office.

This isn't even just true in the United States. In the summer and fall of 2022, protests against religious rules in Iran spread like wildfire. Millions of people, mostly women and girls, took to the streets of Tehran and other cities across Iran to protest rules that make them second-class citizens (if that).[11] It grew to a point where the government, despite their best authoritarian efforts, couldn't stop it. As the *New York Times* put it, "The authorities have tried to crush them with violence and throttle them by disrupting the internet and blocking popular social media platforms such as Instagram. It hasn't worked. Protests have spread from streets to university campuses and to high schools."[12]

Why? Because this generation—your generation—knows how to reach each other digitally and instantly. The powers that be can't track everyone's keystrokes, and the traditional tools used to oppress people just aren't as effective in a digital world.

But rather than having to use technology to circumvent bad politicians and bad laws, what if we could just use the internet to select better politicians with better incentives in the first place? Politicians like Jaylen Smith.

America's Youngest Black Mayor Ever

Jaylen Smith makes Maxwell Frost look old. Smith grew up in Earle, Arkansas, a small city near the Tennessee border. Smith was a good student and could have easily left Earle to attend college in a big city and then pursue a lucrative career from there. Instead, he graduated from high school—and he stayed. Then he ran for mayor—and won. At the age of eighteen, making him the youngest Black mayor in American history.

Why? Because he offered the voters something new—energy, excitement, hope for the future. As City Councilwoman Tyneshia Bohanon said, "He's an asset because he's motivated and he has fresh ideas. He's thinking of others, as he always has. He chose to stay and get his city where he knows it can be."[13]

Now, is Smith a normal teenager? No—he never was. He wore suits to school starting in the ninth grade. He started attending city council meetings, school board meetings, water commission meetings, and community events relentlessly. He showed Earle residents of every age that he cared, he had new ideas, that he was ready to dive into the nitty-gritty of governing. And the people of Earle rewarded his energy and optimism by giving him a chance.[*]

Now, take the Sunrise Movement, a group of young activists trying to fight climate change. The group is best known for its November 2018 protest that led to their occupying House Speaker Nancy Pelosi's office, helping catapult the Green New Deal into the forefront of public attention. The more than 4,000 articles that followed about the Green New Deal mattered, because politicians typically care more about getting attention than anything else.[14] Now, did the Green New Deal happen? No. The bill never even got out of committee.[15]

But when President Biden signed legislation in August 2022, it allocated $369 billion in new funding for climate mitigation projects and investments. The legislation included $128 billion in tax credits for businesses who shift to cleaner forms of energy. Another

---

[*]   In fact, one state over in Texas, eighteen-year-old Joel Castro, a community college student, won a seat on the Alvin City Council in 2018.

$60 billion goes to manufacturing clean energy technology like solar panels and electric vehicles here in the United States. Some experts estimate that the provisions in this one bill alone will help reduce U.S. greenhouse gas emissions by 40 percent by 2030.[16]

The bill passed solely along partisan lines. The Democrats controlled the Senate then solely because Vice President Kamala Harris served as the tie-breaking vote and held a slim, seven-vote majority in the House.

Without the work done by the Sunrise Movement, producing unanimity among Democrats on an issue that had historically been controversial even within the Democratic Party would have been impossible. The members of the Sunrise Movement helped change the cultural and social norms around climate, and that shifted the political incentives enough within the Democratic Party that voting for the most significant climate change legislation ever became a no-brainer for the vast majority of the party. (West Virginia Senator Joe Manchin did hold up the bill because he was worried about hurting the industry—coal mining—that is incredibly important in his state, but he eventually got there.)

Another good example is litigation filed by sixteen young Montanans, arguing that the state constitution guarantees residents the right to a clean and healthful environment and that the state is responsible for maintaining and improving the environment for present and future generations. All of the plaintiffs in *Held v. Montana* are age twenty-two or younger.[17] One witness summed up the issue perfectly: "I have had many, many soccer practices canceled for smoke and heat," he said. "Playing soccer on turf in the heat is miserable. Imagine your feet are boiling in your cleats, burning every single step you take on the field. It burns you out."[18]

And guess what? They won! A Montana district court judge struck down a provision in the Montana Environmental Policy Act that barred the state from considering climate impacts when permitting energy projects. The court also upheld the notion that the right to a clean and healthful environment is guaranteed in the state constitution.[19] Our Children's Trust, the advocacy group that filed the lawsuit, has similar cases pending in Utah, Virginia, Alaska, and Hawaii as well as another—*Juliana v. United States*—in federal court.[20]

These views are shared by young people across the board. A 2021 survey from the Pew Research Center found that younger adults on both sides of the aisle have strong views about issues like climate change. "For example, 49 percent of Gen Z and 48 percent of millennial Republicans (including Republican leaners) say action to reduce the effects of climate change needs to be prioritized today, even if that means fewer resources to deal with other important problems; significantly fewer Gen X (37 percent) and Baby Boomer and older (26 percent) Republicans say the same."[21]

Or let's go back to the issue of abortion. In August 2022, just a few months after the Supreme Court struck down *Roe v. Wade* and made legalizing abortion a state decision, pro-life supporters in Kansas put forth an amendment to the state constitution saying that there was no right to an abortion, that the state had no responsibility to fund abortions, and giving the state the power to prosecute anyone involved in abortions. Kansas is a very conservative state. Everyone expected the amendment to pass easily, especially after supporters were still riding the high of their Supreme Court win just a few months earlier. That's not what happened.

Instead, the proposal lost by nearly twenty points. Why? In large part thanks to Gen Z. How did they do it? By talking to and mobilizing each other and, just like with mobile voting, by using technology.

"The secret to Gen Z's political action," writes *Education Week* in a story arguing that schools can encourage youth activism, "is their ability to mobilize each other. Almost half of the voters aged eighteen to twenty-nine weren't directly contacted by political campaigns in 2020, according to the Tufts research center, but they still managed to have a high turnout in that election. That's because they know how to lean on each other through social media, connecting with community groups and advocating for causes they care about, [Kei] Kawashima-Ginsberg (the director of the Tufts research center) said. That political skill and savvy were on display in the Kansas primary in August, during which voters in the Republican-leaning state rejected an amendment to the state constitution that would have made abortion illegal. Young Kansans used their connections to each other to get organized as a community. Young people in the community organizations worked together to make sure that they were spreading the message about how this particular ballot item could impact their personal life on a daily basis, Kawashima-Ginsberg said. That's an important part of this generation's mobilization style. They're savvy enough about how the political game works."[22]

Let's accept that Kei Kawashima-Ginsberg is right and you

know more than previous generations did when they were your age. Why? Well, while it's easy to disparage social media, it does have an advantage—you receive information a lot faster, and being digitally native has taught you how to automatically scroll through it to find whatever it is you're looking for or are interested in.

Pre-internet, pre-social media, putting together groups of like-minded people took a lot of work. You'd have to post flyers or posters or something physical saying who you were, what you were, that you were having a meeting or an event or something, and practically begging people to join you. You had to rely on someone physically walking by the poster, stopping to read it (or at least slowing down enough to register it), writing down the relevant information, and then showing up somewhere physically at the appointed date and time. Think about how many things have to happen just right for that one little thing to work out. It meant reaching people, spreading information, organizing, even just meeting and talking was much slower, much harder and vastly less efficient.

You know what it sounds a lot like? The way we still vote. And just as platforms like YouTube or TikTok or Discord allow you to instantly reach millions—sometimes even hundreds of millions—of people, imagine what you could do if you could vote that way, too.

Of course the people in charge don't want this. But if you let them keep the single thing that impacts them most—elections—the same as it has always been, your ability to impact and bring about meaningful change on climate, on guns, on immigration, on student loans, on affordable housing, on literally anything is exponentially lower. They'll lie to you and use buzzwords like "security" or "integrity" to keep you in your place. They don't care about any of that. They just care about power—keeping it away from you and for themselves. Don't let them.

You've probably noticed by now that I dislike both political parties. And you also probably noticed that all of the examples in this chapter tend to be issues historically favored by Democrats—gun safety, abortion rights, climate change, student debt, free speech. This should serve as a warning for Republicans. You're ignoring Gen Z at your own peril—especially since so many Gen Z Republicans also want to see real action on issues like climate change.

If you actively oppose mobile voting, you will only push more and more of them (and Gen Alpha) to the other side. The dumb thing is, it's so avoidable. This generation is not particularly partisan. They don't identify themselves in terms of political parties. Rather, they organize around issues that impact their lives. If a good solution is out there to a problem they care about, it doesn't matter to them what party it comes from.

But if only one party is marketing to them, if only one party is trying to organize and activate them in elections, then only one party will benefit. Do you really want to cede an entire generation? That's crazy. Meet them where they are. Just like the Tea Party very effectively used Facebook back in 2010 to organize and counter the inherent advantage Democrats had in turnout thanks to union support, use mobile voting to your advantage. Don't just be the political party yelling at the kids to get off your lawn.

Now, we at the Mobile Voting Project can draft and get bills introduced that would legalize mobile voting in your state. But we can only pass those bills if you get involved. If we can mobilize millions of you across the fifty states, we can change the inputs, scare politicians, and get them to support mobile voting, simply because they've heard from too many of you and the risk of you expressing your displeasure in the next primary is too great. In other words, they shifted because the inputs shifted. And in this case, the inputs are you.

CHAPTER 11

....

HOW YOU CAN
CHANGE THINGS

W e've been together for about 220 pages, and hopefully by now you agree that we both need and deserve
mobile voting. And, if you've made it this far in the
book, while you know that Gen Z and Gen Alpha already have
achieved great things and absolutely can bring mobile voting into
reality, you also know that the deck is stacked against us.

But here's what you may not realize: the status quo—the people
running our politics, our government, our power structures—are
terrified of you. They don't understand how you think. They don't
understand what you care about. They don't understand how you communicate, how you express yourselves, how you see the world. They
know they fucked up your future royally and they're desperate to escape
accountability for it. That's why the last thing they want is to make it
easier for you to vote.

But if you don't force their hand, nothing will change, nothing
will improve, and the future, bleak as it may look today, is going to
be a lot, lot worse by the time they're done destroying the climate,

our democracy, our schools, our healthcare system, and so much else because we know they will always, always, always pick what's better for them personally than what's right morally or substantively.

And guess what? The people who replace them aren't going to be that different. Human nature is human nature. People who desperately need external affirmation and validation, people who aspire to power for the sake of power, are always going to look out for themselves. Rather than expecting human nature to suddenly change or improve, we can deploy the same technology we already use all day, every day, to align their needs and ours.

Because if only a small percentage of voters end up choosing 99 percent of our elected officials, then our elected officials will care only about keeping those small pockets of voters—typically special interests and ideological extremists—happy. But if we can increase primary turnout, even from say 12 percent to 36 percent (so still barely more than a third of eligible voters), then the political inputs shift.

The views and needs of the 36 percent are, by definition, going to represent more of the majority than 12 percent does. That forces politicians to the center. It forces them to prioritize getting things done, not just pointing fingers and getting on TV. And for those elected officials who would like to do something useful, significantly higher primary turnout gives them the cover they need to compromise, to work with the other side, to hear each other out, to find consensus.

But this can only happen if you make it happen. So what does that actually mean?

Here are five ideas for ways to help move the ball forward as we start to introduce legislation in each state to make mobile voting an option. All of this can also be found on mobilevoting.org, along with lots of other tools and resources to turn ideas into action.

1. **TALK TO YOUR FRIENDS.** I'm guessing almost all of them will say, "You're right, why can't we vote on our phones?" And then explain the issue to them. Explain how things currently work and why that results in total dysfunction. Explain what mobile voting is. Explain that the people in charge—and some of the policy groups and academics who unwittingly carry their water—will say it's not secure. Show them that it is. (There's a sample Q & A in Appendix 1 to help guide these exact conversations.) And then ask them to talk to their friends. To post about it. To talk to their classmates, their colleagues, their roommates, their families. The other side will use misinformation as much as they can to suppress your rights, to keep you quiet and out of the way. But when confronted with the truth, their arguments crumble.

2. **JOIN A MOBILE VOTING PROJECT GROUP.** Depending on how active you want to be, we have groups where you can just lend your name and stay informed on what we're up to. Or, if you're really into this, we're organizing groups of supporters in each state so when we introduce legislation, we have a team of people to lobby, testify at hearings, speak at rallies, call legislators, talk to reporters, and all of the other tactics needed to pass legislation that allows mobile voting for all.

3. **BRING THIS INTO YOUR CURRENT GROUPS.** If you're already engaged politically in some way, whether it's activism on

climate or guns or immigration or schools or health care or women's rights or civil rights or anything else, mobile voting makes progress on all of those issues a lot more likely.

In and of itself, mobile voting is just a tool to increase participation and push politicians toward getting things done. But ultimately, it's the key to take so many issues that seem to never get anywhere—like banning assault weapons or creating a carbon tax—and finally change the political inputs so politicians can't keep ignoring reality.

If you're still in school and you're a member of a political organization like the College Democrats or Republicans (or anything else), get them on board. And if you're out of school and involved in local politics in any way, whether by attending community board meetings or knocking on doors for candidates or raising money or hosting meetings or anything else, make this your issue. When the people who care most about politics and policy start demanding change, that matters.

4. **POST ANY OF THESE MESSAGES ON WHATEVER PLATFORMS YOU USE.** Demonstrate your support for mobile voting and get others to start caring about this too. If you scan the QR code below, you'll find sample content for Tik Tok, Instagram, X (formerly known as Twitter), and several other platforms.

5. **PERHAPS MOST IMPORTANT OF ALL, REJECT THE STATUS QUO.** Of course I think mobile voting is the most scalable solution to our problems, but there are lots of good reforms you can support that could help make our democracy more effective. And whether you're active on policy issues or political reforms or just not accepting the line of bullshit you're constantly fed about why things can't change (or are about to be fed about why mobile voting isn't possible), recognize that this world is whatever we make of it. Complaining and pointing fingers doesn't really accomplish anything. And just blaming others for why things are so bad isn't enough.

To be clear, this is really hard. Change always is. Achieving anything worthwhile always is, too. We're lucky to have an incredibly talented team at the Mobile Voting Project, and we've built some really strong alliances (as you saw in the essays in section 4), but it's not like people are flocking to chip in financially or ask how they can help. Calling out the entire system and then creating a real, alternative solution is really risky. This is a pop culture reference from way back, but the empire always strikes back. Always. Fighting for fairness, for what's right, is never easy. Achieving something over the objections of almost everyone in power? Even harder. But what's the alternative? Shrugging your shoulders? Throwing in the towel? Fuck that.

You get one shot at this life. The world is run by the people who care enough to put themselves out there, to speak their minds, to ask others for support and help, to risk being criticized. If you want a better world, a cleaner planet, a safer country, a fairer economy, or anything else, it's on you to make it happen.

That all starts with one small step, one specific action, and it grows from there. I hope you'll choose to make support for mobile voting your one small step, but whatever it is, just do something. Take charge. Reject the status quo. Demand something different, something better.

The future can still be bright. It's up to you. Step up and take it.

APPENDIX 1

WHY MOBILE VOTING?

- Our current approach to voting has left our democracy in crisis.

- Too many voters are left behind. Long lines, inconvenient voting hours, and consolidated polling places force voters to travel farther distances to cast their vote.

- Military and overseas voters, voters with disabilities, and tribal community voters face tremendous obstacles to using traditional voting methods.

- The system was designed to reward hyperpartisanship. Partisan gerrymandering means the eventual winner is chosen at primary elections with turnout averaging below 20 percent. Turnout in local elections is even lower.

- Mobile voting, in addition to other electoral reforms, will help increase turnout in all elections by making voting as convenient as possible and eliminating barriers to voting that continue to impede access to democracy for too many voters.

HOW DOES IT WORK?

- Mobile voting is simply a digital version of paper absentee or mail voting.

- Instead of receiving a ballot by mail, eligible voters can download a voting app from their app store, or with some systems, visit a secure, encrypted website on a phone or other internet-connected device.

- Voters must enter some personally identifiable information, such as name, date of birth, and address or ID number. Then, that information is matched to the voter's registration record to determine which ballot the voter is eligible to vote. This process is similar to the voter lookup used when voting in person or requesting a mail ballot.

- Voters may then mark their ballot on their device. Voters with disabilities can use their assistive technology to read and mark their ballot.

- When finished voting, voters must follow other requirements for mail absentee voting, including signing an affidavit attesting to their identity and providing a photo of an acceptable ID.

- Their completed ballot packet is then encrypted and transmitted using similar cryptographic methods in online banking or commerce. Most mobile voting vendors secure the cast votes on a government cloud system or in a secure system hosted by the state's chief elections official until the local elections office is ready to print them for tabulation.

- Mobile voting does not involve any vote tabulation on the internet.

WHO IS THIS FOR?

- Everyone, but especially voters who face barriers to traditional voting options, including voters with disabilities, military and overseas voters, voters on tribal lands, hospitalized voters, and voters experiencing natural disasters or other emergencies.

IS IT SECURE?

- Yes. It is critical to ensure that every vote in an election is secure, whether cast by hand on paper or using a ballot-marking device, and whether returned in person, by mail, or electronically.

- Security ensures that votes are cast as intended and not tampered with in transit or once received by the election office.

- It is important that any system for voting permits only eligible voters to access and vote their ballots.

- It is also important that voter privacy is protected, regardless of what method a voter uses to vote.

- It is critical that any threat to the voting system is detectable and provides mechanisms to respond and recover.

- In digital voting, voted ballots transmitted electronically are sealed using encryption techniques similar to other secure communication channels like Signal.

- Digital votes can be independently verified so voters can confirm their votes are cast as intended and not tampered with using techniques known as end-to-end verification.

- Digital voting vendors undergo thorough security vetting, including a full corporate infrastructure security review and ongoing penetration testing.

- All digital votes generate a paper ballot for tabulation and to be used in audits or recounts.

HOW ARE BALLOTS TRACKED?

- Votes cast using mobile voting can be tracked using the same process for any other absentee or mail ballot.

- Mobile voting also can offer end-to-end verification to enable voters to confirm their votes are recorded as cast.

WHERE IS IT HAPPENING?

- To date, Tusk Philanthropies and its partners, including the National Cybersecurity Center and National Federation of the Blind, have supported over twenty pilot elections in seven states, including Colorado, Oregon, South Carolina, Utah, Virginia, Washington, and West Virginia. Most pilots involved a mix of military and overseas voters and voters with disabilities.

- Other states have also used mobile voting. In 2020, a total of 330 jurisdictions across eight states used mobile voting, including Alabama, Montana, North Carolina, Oregon, South Carolina, Utah, Washington, and West Virginia. Of those jurisdictions, 103 were in Tusk-supported pilots.

- The pilots helped to demonstrate the impact of mobile voting on participation. In one pilot in King County, Washington, all eligible voters were able to use mobile voting and turnout nearly doubled. A study by the University of Chicago found that turnout among military and overseas voters increased by three to five points in West Virginia in their first statewide election using mobile voting.

- Similarly, turnout in the Arlington County, Virginia, Democratic School Board Caucus jumped by 4 percent after they offered mobile voting in 2021.

WHAT IMPACT DOES THIS HAVE ON OTHER VOTING OPTIONS?

- None. We want to add mobile voting to the other options in place, including in-person voting and vote by mail. Voters should have choices on how to vote and decide which option works for them. We believe by adding mobile voting and making voting even more convenient and easy, more voters will participate in all elections.

HOW DOES IT WORK FOR VOTERS WITH LIMITED BROADBAND ACCESS?

- Expanded access to broadband is and should be a priority to bridge the digital divide. Mobile voting should be available on any smartphone and internet-connected device.

- Expanded access to mobile voting also opens opportunities for election officials to establish secure mobile kiosks for digital remote voting at convenient community locations like grocery stores or public libraries.

HOW DOES IT WORK FOR VOTERS WITH NO SMARTPHONES?

- We believe mobile voting should be an added option for voters but should not remove other options available, including mail ballots and in-person voting.

IT SEEMS DIFFICULT FOR ELECTION OFFICIALS TO IMPLEMENT. WILL IT OVERLY COMPLICATE ELECTION ADMINISTRATION?

- Mobile voting can be incorporated into processes election administrators use for all absentee or mail ballots.

- Mobile voting can also ease the administrative burden of processing military and overseas ballots, which are typically very time-consuming because they may require election officials to send individual emails to voters, and also require election officials to manually transcribe cast votes onto paper ballots for tabulation.

- Mobile voting can make delivering ballots simpler, and most vendors offer the ability to directly print scannable ballots from the digital ballot box, eliminating manual duplication procedures and providing voters with greater assurance their vote will be tabulated as cast.

- In one pilot in Charleston County, South Carolina, the elections office calculated that mobile voting streamlined their processes and saved over 17 hours of staff time.

APPENDIX 2

....

TRADITIONAL AND DIGITAL ABSENTEE VOTING

Comparative Risk Analysis

D igital voting options in U.S. elections are not new. Pilots of various methods of electronic ballot delivery and return have been implemented since the turn of the century. Congress has charged the Department of Defense, through the Federal Voting Assistance Program (FVAP) with studying and developing voting systems to enable military voters serving overseas with the option of returning a ballot via the internet. Early research led to passage of the MOVE Act in 2009, which requires all states to offer electronic transmission of a blank absentee ballot in federal elections to voters who qualify under the Uniformed and Overseas Citizens Absentee Voting Act of 1986 (UOCAVA).

Following passage of the MOVE Act, states passed laws to include electronic ballot-return options for those UOCAVA voters. To date, thirty-two states plus the District of Columbia offer some form of electronic ballot return, including by email, fax, or through a secure web portal, for at least some UOCAVA voters.[1] And more states are expanding eligibility to use electronic ballot delivery and return for voters with disabilities.

Cybersecurity experts have raised concerns about transmitting ballots over the internet due to the inherent cybersecurity risks. In 2013, FVAP undertook an investigation into those risks in the context of traditional mail voting for UOCAVA voters. The study published over a decade ago produced a comparative risk-analysis framework for understanding the risks associated with traditional mail voting and digital voting for certain voters.[2]

Using the model that FVAP developed in its 2013 analysis, we undertook an effort to document the risks associated with the VoteHub mobile voting system our grantees developed. We also performed an updated analysis of the risks associated with traditional by-mail voting systems, particularly given new postal delivery standards and increased use of printing companies for the preparation and transmission of absentee ballots. This summary presents a comparative risk analysis of traditional by-mail voting with the VoteHub system in each phase of the voting process.

VOTING PROCESS DEFINITIONS

Absentee Ballot Preparation

This step includes the preparation of blank absentee ballot packets for delivery to a voter who has requested to vote absentee. This includes the process of confirming a voter's eligibility to vote by absentee ballot in the voter registration database, preparing and printing the correct ballot for the voter's voting precinct, preparing and printing accompanying instructions and forms, and preparing a mailing packet addressed to the voter's ballot mailing address. It may involve sending election and ballot data to a ballot printing and mailing vendor to prepare the absentee packets. In the VoteHub system, it includes the processes of setting up the election in the back-end system, including importing election definition files, ballot PDFs, affidavits, and voter files; conducting logic and accuracy testing; and sealing the digital ballot box by generating the trustee threshold encryption key in the air-gapped Trustee server.

Absentee Ballot Delivery

This step includes the transmission of a blank absentee ballot, ballot affidavit form, and voting instructions to a voter who is voting by mail or absentee. The transmission method may be postal mail or electronic. For the purposes of risk analysis, this process is limited to the time during which the blank absentee ballot materials are outside the hands of either the local election official (LEO) or the voter. In the VoteHub system, this includes the time in which the voting app is communicating via an internet connection to the election official application to look up a voter's registration record, confirm their eligibility, and receive the ballot data that corresponds to the voter's precinct and party (when relevant in a primary election).

Ballot Marking

Ballot marking consists of the voter making selections on a blank ballot, either by hand using ink or through an electronic interface. For the purposes of this risk analysis, this process also includes the additional step by a voter to complete an accompanying affidavit form. The affidavit form may require a voter to provide personally identifiable information, such as a date of birth, last four digits of a social security number, driver's license number, and/or signature. It may also require the voter to provide a photocopy of an acceptable form of ID and/or a witness signature or signatures.

Marked-Ballot Return

This step is the reverse of absentee ballot delivery and involves the transmission of a voted ballot and completed form from the voter to the LEO, either by postal mail or electronic means and according to local requirements and deadlines. The transmission is limited to the time during which the materials are outside the hands of either the voter or the LEO.

Returned Ballot Processing and Tabulation

This process includes:

- Receipt of the voted ballot package by the LEO.

- Absentee ballot verification, including verifying voter's signatures and other required information, verifying timely receipt of the ballot, and verifying the voter was eligible to vote that ballot (e.g., hadn't already submitted a ballot, returned the wrong ballot, etc.).

- Formal acceptance of the ballot for counting and notifying voters eligible to cure any deficiencies on a cast ballot.

- Separating the voter's identifying information from the marked ballot (e.g., removing a voted ballot from an ID envelope).

- Preparing the ballot for scanning and tabulation, including inspecting the ballot for damage or ambiguous marks and, if needed, duplicating the ballot onto ballot stock and in a format that can be read by the election tabulation software.

- Scanning and tabulating the ballots.

APPENDIX 3

....

POST-ELECTION AUDIT

POST-ELECTION AUDIT

This process involves randomly selecting a sufficient number of cast ballots as required by local rules and manually counting them in order to validate that the computerized tallies in the election tabulation system are correct.

Voting-Related Risk Definitions

To create a terminology baseline, certain concepts have been defined.

INTENTIONAL DISRUPTION: Partial or complete stoppage of election systems or processes due to a threat actor knowingly tampering with them.

UNINTENTIONAL ERROR AND ACCIDENTAL DISRUPTION: Partial or complete stoppage of election systems or processes due to unintentional system errors, acts of nature, or third-party outages.

RISK: Risk is the potential for loss, damage, or destruction of assets or data caused by a threat.

TRUST ZONES: Trust zones define points within the voting process where documents or transmissions change hands from owners. In this document, we use four distinct trust zones. In the data flow charts, these are referred to as TZ 1–4. When a ballot or digital transmission changes trust zones, we've assessed potential risks to the processes within. For example, a voter who submits a ballot via mail knows that their ballot is secure up until the point they put it in a ballot drop box; at that point, the ballot moves to TZ2 where the security control shifts to the physical drop box and internal processes of the servicing postal carrier.

- **TRUST ZONE 1 (TZ1)**—The voter.
- **TRUST ZONE 2 (TZ2)**—Mail handlers to include drop boxes and postal service workers; internet service providers and cloud servers, including those hosting the digital ballot box.
- **TRUST ZONE 3 (TZ3)**—Election officials and support staff working within the election office.
- **TRUST ZONE 4 (TZ4)**—Third-party print vendors.

THREAT: A threat exploits a vulnerability and can damage or destroy an asset.

THREAT AGENT: A threat actor or threat agent is a party that is responsible for, or attempts to bring about, harm to an organization.

Threat Terminology

This section provides an overview of terms you will find within this document as it relates to assessed risks to voting processes.

THREAT TERMINOLOGY	DEFINITION	THREAT ACTOR DETAILS
Personally Identifiable Information (PII) Leak	A PII leak is a loss of control, compromise, unauthorized disclosure, unauthorized acquisition, unauthorized access, or any similar term referring to situations where persons other than authorized users have access or potential access to personally identifiable information.	Can be caused accidentally or intentionally by internal or external threat actors.
Spoofing	The act of disguising a communication from an unknown source as being from a known, trusted source to steal information or install malicious software.	Caused intentionally by external threat actors.
Incorrect Input	Refers to either an election official making a data input error into the voter registration database or a voter incorrectly marking a ballot/incorrectly submitted paperwork.	Caused unintentionally by legitimate internal election officials or voters.
Identity Theft	The crime of obtaining the personal or financial information of another person to use their identity to commit fraud.	Caused intentionally by external threat actors.
Denial of Service	An interruption in an authorized user's access to a computer network, typically one caused with malicious intent.	Can be caused unintentionally or intentionally by internal or external threat actors.
Vulnerable Transport Protocol	Weak encryption used for transmitting data digitally that can be captured and read.	Can be caused unintentionally by internal election administrators.
Malware	Software that is specifically designed to disrupt, damage, or gain unauthorized access to a computer system.	Can be caused unintentionally or intentionally by internal or external threat actors.

THREAT TERMINOLOGY	DEFINITION	THREAT ACTOR DETAILS
Resource Exhaustion	Exploits that interfere with election officials' or mail carriers' abilities to move or adjudicate ballots or election-related material.	Can be caused unintentionally or intentionally by external threat actors.
Mail Mishandling	Failing to follow proper procedures to securely receive, sort, transport, and deliver ballots or election-related materials.	Can be caused unintentionally or intentionally by internal threat actors.
Technical Error	Unintentional hardware or software error that can cause a system to malfunction.	Caused unintentionally by internal software.
Resource Risk	Inability to source paper, ink, human resources, or any other resource required to adjudicate, transmit, or transport ballots or election-related material.	Caused unintentionally by external threats.
Email Breach	An incident where the security of an email or associated accounts was compromised.	Caused intentionally by external threat actors.
Tampering	Interfering to cause damage or make unauthorized alterations.	Caused intentionally by external or internal threat actors.
Insider Attack	An insider threat is any employee, vendor, executive, contractor, or other person who works directly with an organization who uses their legitimate access to damage the organization.	Caused intentionally by internal threat actor.
Accessibility	The inability for a voter to receive, mark, review, or remediate issues with ballots or election-related documents due to location, disabilities, or disaster events.	Caused unintentionally by external threats.
Voter Coercion	Persuading a voter to vote for a candidate they otherwise would not have voted for by use of force or bribery.	Caused intentionally by external threat actors.
Multiple Ballot Submissions	Illegally submitting multiple ballots.	Caused intentionally by external or internal threat actors.

THREAT TERMINOLOGY	DEFINITION	THREAT ACTOR DETAILS
Ballot Destruction or Theft	Removing legitimate ballots from legitimate transport channels.	Caused intentionally by internal or external threat actors.
Illegitimate Reporting	Election officials in charge of reporting election results knowingly report incorrect numbers to the public.	Caused intentionally by internal threat actors.

COMPARATIVE RISK ANALYSIS

Absentee Ballot Preparation

ANALYSIS: Overall, the risks in absentee ballot preparation are low in both traditional absentee voting and VoteHub. With the expansion of automatic and permanent vote-by-mail options, and the increased use of ballot-on-demand printing, it is worth considering the risks in voter registration data file transfers to third-party software and vendors, as well as the risks of insider attacks and unintentional errors when LEOs manually prepare absentee ballot packages.

TRADITIONAL ABSENTEE VOTING SYSTEM			
VOTING STEP	TRUST ZONE	THREAT VECTOR/THREAT	MITIGATIONS
Data File Transfer	3 and 4	Intentional attack or unintentional error.	Internal controls.
		Data files including ballot files, instructions, envelope art, and voter lists may be corrupted, modified, or destroyed in transit to the print facility.	
Ballot Printing	3 and 4	Intentional attack or unintentional error.	Internal controls.
		Third-party vendors or election officials can intentionally or unintentionally destroy or misprint ballots.	

TRADITIONAL ABSENTEE VOTING SYSTEM

VOTING STEP	TRUST ZONE	THREAT VECTOR/THREAT	MITIGATIONS
Ballot Printing	3 and 4	Unintentional error.	Purchase required materials well in advance of elections.
		Resource risk: EOs or vendors in charge of printing ballots may run out of necessary resources to print ballots and materials.	
Ballot Package Assembly	3 and 4	Unintentional error.	Internal controls.
		Third-party vendors or election officials can unintentionally assemble the wrong ballot materials for voters, including the wrong precinct or party ballot style, wrong instructions, or wrong mailing address.	

VOTEHUB MOBILE VOTING SYSTEM

VOTING STEP	TRUST ZONE	THREAT VECTOR/THREAT	MITIGATIONS
Data File Transfer	3	Intentional attack or unintentional error.	Automatic data integrity checks; logic and accuracy testing.
		Data files including ballot files, election definition files, affidavits, and voter registration data may be corrupted, modified, or destroyed when uploading to the EO application.	
Sealing the Digital Ballot Box	3	Intentional attack.	Internal controls; physical access controls; air-gapped trustee application; threshold encryption.
		A corrupt trustee or trustees charged with creating ballot encryption keys and sealing the digital ballot box may result in a leaked or lost decryption key or keys.	
Election Setup	3	Intentional attack.	Use of dynamic DNS servers and use of DDoS vendors like Cloudflare, Arbor, etc.
		Denial of service: A denial of service attack on the back-end server hosting the EO application and digital ballot box may prevent the EO from successfully completing the election setup process.	

Absentee Ballot Delivery

ANALYSIS: Absentee ballot delivery has been seen as a relatively low-risk process for both digital and mail-in voting options with most of the risk stemming from insecure transmission mechanisms.[1] Our analysis expanded on the idea by also including risks related to physical transportation methods, which can be strained when delivering ballots overseas or into areas during a disaster. Recent changes within the United States Postal Service (USPS) have weakened its ability to speedily transport mail. One example of a change is the difference in postal delivery mailing standards, as noted previously.

TRADITIONAL ABSENTEE VOTING SYSTEM			
VOTING STEP	**TRUST ZONE**	**THREAT VECTOR /THREAT**	**MITIGATIONS**
Ballot Transported to USPS	2	Intentional attack or unintentional error.	Internal controls, mail tracking codes.
		Mail mishandling: Mail can be accidentally or intentionally dropped, lost, or damaged during pickup, sorting, and transport.	
Internal Mail Process	2	Intentional attack or unintentional error.	Internal controls, mail tracking codes.
		Mail mishandling: Mail can be accidentally or intentionally dropped, lost, or damaged during pickup, sorting, and transport.	
Mail Delivered to Voter	2	Intentional attack or unintentional error.	Internal controls, mail tracking codes.
		Mail mishandling: Mail can be accidentally or intentionally dropped, lost, or damaged during pickup, sorting, and transport.	
Transport	2	Intentional attack or unintentional error.	Internal resource acquisition and hiring processes that front-load resources early.
		Resource exhaustion: Slowdowns in commodity or personnel resources required to alert voters to their absentee status can prevent a voter from responding to rejections in an appropriate amount of time.	

VOTEHUB MOBILE VOTING SYSTEM			
VOTING STEP	**TRUST ZONE**	**THREAT VECTOR /THREAT**	**MITIGATIONS**
Download Application	2	Intentional attack. Spoofed application: A voter may download and install a fake application that could infect the device with malware or steal input information.	Relay download link directly to voters via email or the official state or county website. Only host applications on verified application stores from Google and Apple. Actively work with law enforcement and hosting providers to remove spoofed applications.
Voter Lookup and Ballot Delivery	2	Unintentional error. A loss of internet connection may prevent the VoteHub app from communicating to the back-end server during the voter lookup and ballot delivery phase of voting while using the app.	Instructions in the app will direct the voter to troubleshoot internet connection.
Voter Lookup and Ballot Delivery	2	Intentional attack. A denial of service attack on the voting app and/or back-end server may prevent the app from communicating during the voter lookup and ballot delivery phase of voting while using the app.	Use of dynamic DNS servers and use of DDoS vendors like Cloudflare, Arbor, etc.
Voter Lookup and Digital Ballot Delivery	1	Intentional attack. Voter impersonation: An attacker could impersonate a legitimate voter and falsely access and mark a voter's ballot.	Signature verification by election officials to verify eligible voter submitted physical ballot if using physical return; use of time-expiring one-time access code to the voter's email address in voter registry for authorization to use digital return.

Ballot Marking

ANALYSIS: The greatest risks associated with marking are voter coercion/vote buying or interception of a ballot by the incorrect person. In its comparative risk analysis of both traditional and digital absentee voting systems, the FVAP found this risk to be higher for physical marking and lower for electronic marking due to unintentional errors in hand marking a ballot that are mitigated with digital ballot-marking systems. The VoteHub system further lowers the risk of incorrect marking by allowing a voter to go back and change their choices before submitting and by providing a means to authenticate with the application using PII and a one-time access code to lower the chance of interception by an unauthorized party. The application also allows for a print-at-home option of the completed ballot and affidavit that would allow states to save money on initial physical delivery and provide a more accessible option to voters overseas or those who have difficulties receiving mail unassisted.

TRADITIONAL ABSENTEE VOTING SYSTEM

VOTING STEP	TRUST ZONE	THREAT VECTOR /THREAT	MITIGATIONS
Ballot Marking	1	Unintentional error.	Clear instructions delivered along with ballots.
		Incorrect marking: A voter incorrectly fills in selection bubbles.	
Ballot Marking	1	Unintentional error.	Clear instructions and design of the form; curing process to enable voters to correct errors.
		Error on signature affidavit: A voter incorrectly completes the ballot affidavit document.	
Ballot Marking	1	Unintentional error.	None.
		Accessibility: Voters may be unable to hand-mark a ballot due to visual or physical limitations.	
Ballot Marking	1	Intentional attack.	Election official education outreach and proper instructions; engaging law enforcement.
		Voter coercion: A voter may be paid or forced to make contest choices.	

VOTEHUB MOBILE VOTING SYSTEM

VOTING STEP	TRUST ZONE	THREAT VECTOR /THREAT	MITIGATIONS
Ballot Marking	1	Intentional attack. Malware on device: Malware on the voter's device may spy on user inputs to steal information or attempt to change the voter's contest choices.	Detection and response capabilities via ballot checking process, especially when conducted on a separate device. Code signing and trusted signing of application integrations. Application sandboxing. Print-at-home functionality. Latest system update required for application use. Ability to report an error to LEO for remediation.
Ballot Marking	1	Intentional attack. Voter coercion: A voter may be paid or forced to make contest choices.	Permit voters to submit multiple ballots digitally and count only the last one submitted; election official education outreach and proper instructions; engaging law enforcement.
Ballot Checking	2	Intentional attack. Malware on supporting infrastructure: Malware located on the device used by the voter performing a ballot check or on the verification site can prevent a voter checking their ballot. Malware on the infrastructure may also spread malware to other devices or steal user information.	Encourage voters to use a separate device when performing a ballot check.
Ballot Checking	2	Intentional attack. Malware on verification site: Malware located on the verification site can prevent a voter checking their ballot.	Encourage multiple verification sites for each election; pairing code verification process provides tools to authenticate verification sites; conduct ongoing penetration testing and system hardening.
Ballot Checking	1	Intentional attack or unintentional error. Dispute resolution: Voter may mistakenly or intentionally misreport a problem during the ballot check, making a false claim that the voting software altered their vote.	Provide voter with alternative voting options; provide voter with multiple verification sites.

VOTEHUB MOBILE VOTING SYSTEM

VOTING STEP	TRUST ZONE	THREAT VECTOR /THREAT	MITIGATIONS
Digital Return Authorization	1	Intentional attack. Email breached: If an attacker has access to the voter's email address on record in the voter registration database, they can intercept the time-limited one-time passcode needed to authorize a digital ballot submission.	Encryption of email addresses. Provide a set expiry window for one-time codes; signature verification process to verify eligible voter. submitted the digital ballot.
Digital Return Authorization	2	Intentional attack. Malware on supporting infrastructure: Malware located on the one-time access-code servers can prevent a voter from completing the digital ballot submission authorization process. Malware on the infrastructure may also spread malware to other devices or steal user information.	Offer the physical return option to voters as a backup. Implement the system into a hardened environment with common cyber tools. Harden backend systems. Performing vulnerability assessments and penetration tests to identify vulnerabilities.
Digital Return Authorization	2	Intentional attack or unintentional error. Denial of service or network error: A denial of service attack on the infrastructure supporting the one-time access code and digital return authorization process may prevent a voter from completing the authorization process. The voter may also experience a loss of internet connection during this process that prevents them from successfully completing this step.	Use of dynamic DNS and DDoS protection services like Cloudflare, Arbor, etc., to prevent a successful DoS attack; offer voter to use physical ballot return.

Marked-Ballot Return

ANALYSIS: The threats to mail return are largely related to ballot mishandling during transport and inefficiencies in USPS transport that can lead to slowdowns. Electronic return has separate threats mostly related to technical errors of devices. The trade-off in increased risks with absentee voting are the gains in accessibility given to disadvantaged groups in both cases. In 2020, nearly 62 percent of people with disabilities voted, up from 56 percent in 2016. Of that number, more than 53 percent of voters with disabilities voted by mail.[2] This number can be increased even further by providing a digital option that can support voters with vision or print disabilities that make voting and handling paper ballots impossible.

TRADITIONAL ABSENTEE VOTING SYSTEM

VOTING STEP	TRUST ZONE	THREAT VECTOR/THREAT	MITIGATIONS
Mail Transported	2	Intentional attack or unintentional error.	Internal controls, mail tracking codes.
		Mail mishandling: Mail can be accidentally or intentionally dropped, lost, or damaged during pickup, sorting, and transport.	

VOTEHUB MOBILE VOTING SYSTEM

VOTING STEP	TRUST ZONE	THREAT VECTOR/THREAT	MITIGATIONS
Voter Digitally Submits Ballot	2	Intentional attack or unintentional error.	Use of dynamic DNS and DDoS protection services like Cloudflare, Arbor, etc., to prevent a successful DoS attack; voter verification of a successful ballot submission through the use of a ballot tracking code and public verification site; offer voter to use physical ballot return.
		Denial of service or network error: A denial of service attack on the servers and infrastructure supporting the digital ballot box or the VoteHub app may prevent a voter from completing the authorization process. The voter may also experience a loss of internet connection during this process that prevents them from successfully completing this step.	
Voter Digitally Submits Ballot	1	Intentional attack or unintentional error.	The system is natively configurable to only allow one ballot submission per voter; election official procedures to ensure only one ballot is counted per voter.
		Multiple ballot submissions: A voter could intentionally or unintentionally use the application to submit multiple ballots.	

VOTEHUB MOBILE VOTING SYSTEM			
VOTING STEP	**TRUST ZONE**	**THREAT VECTOR/THREAT**	**MITIGATIONS**
Voter Digitally Submits Ballot	1	Intentional attack. Man in the middle: Communication between the voter device and the digital ballot box may be intercepted or modified in transit.	The system uses open-source and publicly verified cryptographic protocols for data transmission and storage outlined in NIST SP 800–175 and PKSC; voter has the option to verify the ballot submission is correct through the use of the ballot tracking code on the public verification site.

Returned Ballot Processing and Tabulation

ANALYSIS: Ballot processing shares comparable threats between physical delivery and electronic methods because both systems rely on physical paper ballots. Ballots are received and sorted, and signatures and supporting documents are assessed to determine the validity of the ballot. Approved ballots are scanned and tabulated before results are reported to the public. With electronic ballots, signature and supporting-document verification is performed digitally. Approved ballots are moved offline to an air-gapped environment, decrypted, and printed before being scanned and tabulated. Primary risks for both options include ballot mishandling or insider threats. Additionally, electronic systems are subject to technical failures.

TRADITIONAL ABSENTEE VOTING SYSTEM			
VOTING STEP	**TRUST ZONE**	**THREAT VECTOR/THREAT**	**MITIGATIONS**
Signature Verification	3	Intentional attack or unintentional error. Ballot mishandling: Election officials could intentionally or unintentionally fail to follow internal processes. This could lead to absentee ballots not being counted.	Internal election official processes.

TRADITIONAL ABSENTEE VOTING SYSTEM

VOTING STEP	TRUST ZONE	THREAT VECTOR/THREAT	MITIGATIONS
Signature Verification	3	Intentional attack or unintentional error. False negatives: A legitimate ballot could be deemed illegitimate for a multitude of reasons and not counted.	Internal election official processes.
Signature Verification	3	Intentional attack or unintentional error. False positives: An illegitimate ballot could be deemed legitimate for a multitude of reasons and be counted.	Internal election official processes.
EO Adjudication Message	3	Intentional attack or unintentional error. Denial of service: Attacks against ballot tracking systems and websites can prevent a user from being alerted to their acceptance or rejection status.	Dynamic DNS and DDoS protection services; mailing notifications of ballot status.
Ballot Storage	3	Accidental disruption or intentional attack. Ballot destruction: An accident, natural disaster, or intentional physical attack on the physical location at which physical ballots are stored could lead to the destruction of cast ballots.	Preprocessing of absentee ballots, including scanning paper ballots, with backups of the ballot images stored off-site.
Ballot Storage	3	Intentional attack. Ballot destruction or theft: A threat actor who has access to ballot processing and storage can misplace or destroy cast ballots.	Internal election official processes; physical security measures.
Ballot Scanning	3	Unintentional error. Technical error: Devices used to scan ballots can experience a fault, causing contest selections to be under- or over-counted.	Internal election official processes; post-election audits.
Ballot Scanning	3	Unintentional error. Machine failure: Devices used to scan ballots can experience malfunctions or breakdowns that slow or even stop ballot tabulation and lead to slower election results reporting.	Internal election official processes; backup equipment.

TRADITIONAL ABSENTEE VOTING SYSTEM

VOTING STEP	TRUST ZONE	THREAT VECTOR/THREAT	MITIGATIONS
Ballot Adjudication	3	Intentional attack or unintentional error. Ballots subject to adjudication to determine voter intent could be intentionally or accidentally adjudicated incorrectly, resulting in a vote counting in a way that does not reflect the voter's intent.	Internal election processes, including bipartisan adjudication teams; post-election audits.
Results Reporting	3	Intentional attack or unintentional error. Illegitimate reporting: Election officials charged with conveying the election results to the public can report false numbers either intentionally or unintentionally.	External and internal audits.
Results Reporting	3	Intentional attack. Denial of service attack on election reporting sites: A denial of service attack may disrupt the ability for the public to access election results on public reporting websites.	Dynamic DNS and DDoS protection services; physically posting election results in election offices.

VOTEHUB MOBILE VOTING SYSTEM

VOTING STEP	TRUST ZONE	THREAT VECTOR/THREAT	MITIGATIONS
Signature Verification	3	Intentional attack or unintentional error. Ballot mishandling: Election officials could intentionally or unintentionally fail to follow internal processes. This could lead to digital absentee ballots not being counted.	Publicly available cryptographic records of all ballots cast on the digital bulletin board. Internal election official processes.
Signature Verification	3	Intentional attack or unintentional error. False negatives: A legitimate ballot could be deemed illegitimate for a multitude of reasons and not counted.	Internal election official processes.

VOTEHUB MOBILE VOTING SYSTEM

VOTING STEP	TRUST ZONE	THREAT VECTOR/THREAT	MITIGATIONS
Signature Verification	3	Intentional attack or unintentional error. False positives: An illegitimate ballot could be deemed legitimate for a multitude of reasons and be counted.	Internal election official processes.
EO Adjudication Message	2	Intentional attack or unintentional error. Denial of service: Attacks against ballot tracking services and digital return infrastructure can prevent a user from being alerted to their acceptance or rejection status.	Dynamic DNS and DDoS protection services; mailing notifications of ballot status.
Ballot Storage	2	Intentional attack. Malware on servers: Malware on server infrastructure may attempt to disrupt election infrastructure or attempt to secretly modify votes.	Publicly viewable digital ledger shows all transactions to the digital ballot box. Items hosted within a digital ballot box encrypted at rest. Hash chain in use to validate items appended to digital ballot box and bulletin board. Ballots are decrypted, printed, and scanned for tabulation in air-gapped environment.
Ballot Storage	3	Unintentional disruption or intentional attack. Ballot destruction: An accident, natural disaster, or intentional physical attack on the physical location at which physical ballots are stored could lead to the destruction of cast ballots.	Encrypted digital ballots remain as backups in the digital ballot box.
Ballot Storage	3	Intentional attack. Ballot destruction or theft: A threat actor who has access to ballot storage can obstruct the election process by disrupting normal server function.	Internal election official processes; physical security measures.

VOTEHUB MOBILE VOTING SYSTEM

VOTING STEP	TRUST ZONE	THREAT VECTOR/THREAT	MITIGATIONS
Ballot Printing	4	Unintentional error. Machine failure: Software and equipment used to print scannable ballots following ballot decryption can experience technical errors that prevent ballots from being printed.	EOs can manually duplicate digital ballots onto scannable ballots for tabulation; maintaining backup equipment.
Ballot Scanning	3	Unintentional error. Technical error: Devices used to scan ballots can experience a fault, causing contest selections to be under- or over-counted.	Logic and accuracy testing. Audits.
Ballot Scanning	3	Unintentional error. Machine failure: Devices used to scan ballots can experience malfunctions or breakdowns that slow or even stop ballot tabulation and lead to slower election results reporting.	Internal election official processes; backup equipment.
Results Reporting	3	Intentional attack or unintentional error. Illegitimate reporting: Election officials charged with conveying the election results to the public can report false numbers either intentionally or unintentionally.	Internal EO processes. External and internal audits.
Results Reporting	3	Intentional attack. Denial of service attack on election reporting sites: A denial of service attack may disrupt the ability for the public to access election results on public reporting websites.	Dynamic DNS and DDoS protection services; physically posting election results in election offices.

Post-Election Audit

ANALYSIS: Both systems rely on physical paper ballots for tabulation and auditing purposes and share a similar risk. In its report in 2013, the FVAP found virtually no additional risk to this step.[3] An added benefit of the electronic voting system is that along with a physical paper trail, there is a publicly verifiable digital ledger that cannot be broken for each ballot submitted. This feature preventively detects unauthorized items being added to the digital ballot box and provides a secondary form of auditing material on top of the already generated paper ballots.

Summary

The following table shows the overall presence of a known security risk identified by our internal assessment of security methods for both paper absentee voting and electronic voting methods. Our internal review of security threats and controls fell in line with the FVAP results stating that both electronic and mail-in methods of absentee voting were relatively comparable in overall risks associated with threats. Our assessment did not include a quantitative assessment of risk impact, but the improved controls outlined further in the assessment lead our team to assess our mobile voting technology as a more secure method of voting in comparison to the electronic absentee voting system studied in the 2013 FVAP report, and an equally or more secure method of voting for certain populations compared to traditional mail-in methods.

COMPARATIVE ANALYSIS

THREAT	ELECTRONIC VOTING PRESENT?	PAPER ABSENTEE PRESENT?
PII Leak	Yes	Yes
Spoofed Website/Number	Yes	Yes
Incorrect Input	Yes	Yes
Identity Theft	Yes	Yes
Vulnerable Transport Protocol	Yes	Yes
Malware on Server	Yes	No
Mail Mishandling	No	Yes
Resource Exhaustion	Yes	Yes
Denial of Service	Yes	Yes
Technical Error	Yes	Yes
Resource Risk	No	Yes
Data File Tampering	No	Yes
Spoofing	Yes	Yes
Incorrect Marking	No	Yes
Accessibility	No	Yes
Voter Coercion	Yes	Yes
Malware on Device	Yes	No

THREAT	ELECTRONIC VOTING PRESENT?	PAPER ABSENTEE PRESENT?
Email Breach	Yes	No
Malware on Supporting Infrastructure	Yes	Yes
Multiple Ballot Submissions	Yes	Yes
Ballot Destruction or Theft	Yes	Yes
Man in the Middle	Yes	No
False Positives	Yes	Yes
False Negatives	Yes	Yes
Illegitimate Reporting	Yes	Yes

Providing voting options that are accessible for all eligible voters who are unable to vote via traditional methods is important to our representative democracy. Our election system works best when all voters who can vote do, and this research and development project is moving the ball forward to ensure that initiative becomes a reality.

ACKNOWLEDGMENTS

This was not an easy book to write and there are a lot of people to thank here. I was fortunate to work with really incredible editors—Anna Michels and Liv Turner—at Sourcebooks, and I'm also grateful to Dominique Raccah, Sourcebooks CEO, for encouraging me to write this book. Thanks, as always, to my great agent, Kirsten Neuhaus.

There are a lot of people to thank from both the Tusk Holdings world and the Mobile Voting Project. For help with this book itself, I owe a tremendous deck of gratitude to Meaghan Collins, Bob Greenlee, Jocelyn Bucaro, Tristine Skyler, Hugo Lindgren, Cory Epstein, Basil Apostolo, Chelsea Huff, and Noa Kasman. Thank you to everyone who contributed essays for this book including my very close friend and brother-in-law, Josh Gottheimer, as well as David Hogg, Martin Luther King III, Cisco Aguilar, Maurice Turner, Katherine Gehl, Rob Ritchie, Avalon Zborovsky-Fenster, and Mark Riccobono.

More broadly, mobile voting is the hardest issue I've ever

worked on. In addition to everyone I've mentioned, special thanks to Sheila Nix, Mac Warner, Joe Brotherton, Bryan Finney, Nimit Sawhney, Maurice Turner, Joe Kiniry, Reuben Broadfoot, Drake Rambke, Aileen Kim, Sam Polstein, Ricky Soto, Evan Brot, Noma Shields, Malcom Robbs, Dara Freed, Ven Medabalmi, Arndrea Waters King, Sam Kinch, Stephen Mogle, John Sebes, Greg Miller, Anne O'Flaherty, Linda Rebrovick, Jacob Gyldenkærne, Camilla Banja, Emil Kampp, Lukas Andrade, Sebastian Berendt, Stefan Patachi, Maria Petersen, Sara Janackova, Keith Luchtel, Barret Anspach, Chris Borgea, Eliza Hubbard, Eliot Adams, Eli Zibin, Lou Ann Blake, Isaac Cramer, Josh Daniels, Jeff Ellington, Jeff Kaloc, Jay Kaplan, Amber McReynolds, Clark Rachfal, Forrest Senti, Sarah Streyder, Chris Walker, Chuck Flannery, Donald Kersey, Brittany Westfall, Amelia Powers Gardner, Rozan Mitchell, Dan Lonai, Lori Augino, Diane Robinson, Rebecca Nowatchik, Michelle Bishop, Curtis Chong, Jim Sandstrum, Jim Gashel, Sarah Blahovec, John Pare, Ava Mateo, Zev Shapiro, Nick Delis, Thanasi Dilos, Anjelica Smith, Tappan Vickory, Chris Tallent, Wade Henderson, Sam Oliker-Friedland, Jake Matilsky, Katie Usalis, Todd Connor, Eric Bronner, Miles Rapoport, Nathan Lockwood, Andy Moore, Ramon Perez, Eric Starr, Miles Taylor, RC Carter, Whitney Quesenbery, Island Pinnick, Felicia Erlich, Jamil Jaffer, Judd Choate, Trevor Timmons, Michael Walker, Josh Graham Lynn, Matt Snider, Claire Stanley, and Spencer Overton.

Thank you to all of the people who taught me everything I needed to know about politics, technology, and how to bring the two together including Mike Bloomberg, Howard Wolfson, Patti Harris, Kevin Sheekey, Ed Skyler, Mike Lynch, Travis Kalanick,

Christian Genetski, Jim Kessler, Josh Isay, Jef Pollack, Micah Lasher, Henry Stern, Parke Spencer, Ron Stack, John Filan, Luis Saenz, and so, so many others.

NOTES

....

CHAPTER 1

1 Lee Drutman, "How Much Longer Can This Era of Political Gridlock Last?" FiveThirtyEight, March 4, 2021, https://fivethirtyeight.com/features/how-much-longer-can-this-era-of-political-gridlock-last/.

2 Taylor Mooney, Lilia Luciano, and Justin Sherman, "Texas Laws Allow Teachers to Carry Guns on School Grounds with Little Regulation," CBS News, November 17, 2022, https://www.cbsnews.com/news/texas-teachers-guns-at-school; "California Requires Gender-Neutral Displays for Toys and Childcare Items at Large Stores," CBS News, October 11, 2021, https://www.cbsnews.com/news/california-law-gender-neutral-toy-displays-department-stores/.

3 Joshua Ferrer and Michael Thorning, "2022 Primary Turnout: Trends and Lessons for Boosting Participation Report," Bipartisan Policy Center, March 9, 2023, https://bipartisanpolicy.org/download/?file=/wp-content/uploads/2023/03/Primary-Turnout-Report_R03.pdf.

4 Joe Drape and Jacqueline Williams. "FanDuel and DraftKings Employees Bet at Rival Sites." New York Times, October 6, 2015, https://www.nytimes.com/2015/10/06/sports/fanduel-draftkings-fantasy-employees-bet-rivals.html.

5 "Attorney General Announces Settlement with Fantasy Sports Companies to Cease Their Operations in Alabama," Office of the Attorney General, State of Alabama, April 29, 2016, https://www.alabamaag.gov/wp-content/uploads/2023/05/827.pdf; Associated Press, "Delaware Attorney General

Orders End to Online Fantasy Sports Betting," NBC 10, Philadelphia, July 9, 2016, https://www.nbcphiladelphia.com/news/sports/delaware-attorney -general-orders-end-to-online-fantasy-sports-betting/2030445/; *Honolulu Star-Advertiser* Staff, "Honolulu Prosecutor Tells Fantasy Sports Companies to Cease and Desist," *Honolulu Star-Advertiser*, February 2, 2016, https:// www.staradvertiser.com/2016/02/02/breaking-news/honolulu-prosecutor -tells-fantasy-sports-companies-to-cease-and-desist/; Walt Bogdanich, Joe Drape, and Jacqueline Williams, "New York Attorney General Tells Fantasy Sites to Stop Taking Bets," *New York Times*, November 10, 2015, https:// www.nytimes.com/2015/11/11/sports/football/draftkings-fanduel-new-york -attorney-general-tells-fantasy-sites-to-stop-taking-bets-in-new-york.html.

CHAPTER 2

1   Shawn Zeller, "No Quarter for Centrists in House: 2020 Vote Studies," Roll Call, March 3, 2021, https://rollcall.com/2021/03/03/no-quarter-for -centrists-in-house-2020-vote-studies/.

2   Joshua Ferrer and Michael Thorning, "2022 Primary Turnout: Trends and Lessons for Boosting Participation Report," Bipartisan Policy Center, March 2023, 9, https://bipartisanpolicy.org/download/?file=/wp-content/uploads /2023/03/Primary-Turnout-Report_R03.pdf.

3   Morning Consult + Politico, "National Tracking Poll, Project 2205161," May 2022, https://www.politico.com/f/?id=00000180-fe72-d0c2-a9ae -ff7250f80000&nname=playbook&nid=0000014f-1646-d88f-a1cf -5f46b7bd0000&nrid=0000014e-f115-dd93-ad7f-f91513e50001&nlid= 630318.

CHAPTER 3

1   Joe Hasell, "Why Do Far Fewer People Die in Famines Today?" Our World in Data, 2018, http://ourworldindata.org/why-do-far-fewer-people-die-in -famines-today.

2   Sarah Best, "'If It Bleed, It Leads'—The Modern Implications of an Outdated Phrase," *Pepperdine University Graphic*, May 9, 2021, https://pepperdine -graphic.com/opinion-if-it-bleeds-it-leads-the-modern-implications-of-an -outdated-phrase/.

3   Telecommunications Act of 1996, 47 U,S.C. § 230, U.S. Government

Publishing Office, 2021, accessed August 10, 2023, https://www.govinfo.gov
/content/pkg/USCODE-2021-title47/pdf/USCODE-2021-title47-chap5
-subchapII-partI-sec230.pdf.

4   Derek Thompson, "Click Here If You Want to Be Sad," *The Atlantic*, March 24,
2023, https://www.theatlantic.com/newsletters/archive/2023/03/negativity
-bias-online-news-consumption/673499/.

5   Laura Hautala, "Can Facebook, Mark Zuckerberg, New Hires Take On Troll
Farms and Data Privacy After Cambridge Analytica?" CNET, April 11, 2018,
https://www.cnet.com/news/privacy/can-facebook-mark-zuckerberg-new
-hires-take-on-troll-farms-and-data-privacy-after-cambridge-analytica/.

6   "Vietnam: 1965–1975," *Mass Atrocity Endings* (blog), World Peace
Foundation, Fletcher School, Tufts University, August 7, 2015, https://sites
.tufts.edu/atrocityendings/2015/08/07/vietnam-vietnam-war/.

7   "Public Trust in Government 1958–2022," Pew Research Center, September
19, 2023, https://www.pewresearch.org/politics/2023/09/19/public-trust-in
-government-1958–2023/.

8   Esteban Ortiz-Ospina, "The Rise of Social Media," Our World in Data, 2019,
accessed August 10, 2023, https://ourworldindata.org/rise-of-social-media.

9   David Neiwert, "Conspiracy Meta-Theory 'The Storm' Pushes The
'Alternative' Envelope Yet Again," Southern Poverty Law Center, January 17,
2018, https://www.splcenter.org/hatewatch/2018/01/17/conspiracy-meta
-theory-storm-pushes-alternative-envelope-yet-again.

10   Rachel Treisman, "Georgia Officials Fact-Check an Infamous Trump Phone
Call in Real Time," National Public Radio, June 21, 2022, https://www.npr
.org/2022/06/21/1106472863/georgia-officials-fact-check-infamous-trump
-phone-call-in-real-time.

11   Domenico Montanaro, "Senate Acquits Trump in Impeachment Trial—
Again," National Public Radio, February 13, 2021, https://www.npr.org
/sections/trump-impeachment-trial-live-updates/2021/02/13/967098840
/senate-acquits-trump-in-impeachment-trial-again.

CHAPTER 4

1   "Former New York State Senator Chris Jacobs," New York State Senate,
NYSenate.gov, accessed September 14, 2023, https://www.nysenate.gov
/senators/chris-jacobs.

2   National Rifle Association Political Victory Fund. 2020. "Your Vote Defends Freedom!—Please Vote Chris Jacobs for U.S. House!" accessed September 5, 2023, https://www.nrapvf.org/emails/2020/new-york/chris-jacobs-ny-27 -general/.

3   Associated Press, "Buffalo Supermarket Shooting: What Do We Know So Far?," May 18, 2022, https://apnews.com/article/buffalo-shooting-what-to -know-bcb5e0bd2aedb925d20440c2005ffef8.

4   Zoë Richards, "GOP Lawmaker Calls It Quits after Being 'Annihilated' for Backing Gun Control," NBC News, June 3, 2022, https://www.nbcnews.com /politics/2022-election/gop-lawmaker-calls-quits-annihilated-backing-gun -control-rcna31922/.

5   Nicholas Fandos and Jesse McKinley, "N.Y. Republican Drops Re-Election Bid After Bucking His Party on Guns," June 3, 2022, *New York Times*, https:// www.nytimes.com/2022/06/03/nyregion/chris-jacobs-congress-guns.html.

6   Steve Inskeep, "Republican Rep. Jacobs Won't Seek Reelection After He Changed His Stance on Guns," NPR, June 17, 2022, https://www.npr.org /2022/06/17/1105790882/republican-rep-jacobs-wont-seek-reelection -after-he-changed-his-stance-on-guns.

7   Nick Wingfield, "Amazon Counts Its Suitors: 238 Want to Be Home for 2nd Headquarters," *New York Times*, October 23, 2017, https://www.nytimes.com /2017/10/23/technology/amazon-headquarters.html.

8   Kurt Schlosser, "Tucson Sends a 21-Foot-Tall Cactus to Jeff Bezos with a Message: Amazon Can Grow in Arizona," GeekWire, September 14, 2017, https://www.geekwire.com/2017/tucson-sends-21-foot-tall-cactus-jeff-bezos -message-amazon-can-grow-arizona/.

9   Leanna Garfield, "An HQ2 Finalist Wants to Name a City after Amazon and Create a Highway Called 'Jeff Bezos Parkway,'" *Business Insider*, March 26, 2018, https://www.businessinsider.com/amazon-hq2-atlanta-suburb -stonecrest-bid-2018-3.

10   Matt Day, "Cities Crank Up Publicity Stunts as Amazon's HQ2 Bid Deadline Arrives," *Seattle Times*, October 19, 2017, https://www.seattletimes.com /business/amazon/cities-crank-up-publicity-stunts-as-amazons-hq2-bid -deadline-arrives/.

11   "New New Yorkers Give Amazon A Prime 2–1 Welcome, Quinnipiac University Poll Finds; But Voters Are Divided On Tax Breaks To Make The

Deal" December 5, 2019, Quinnipiac University, https://poll.qu.edu/Poll-Release-Legacy?releaseid=2589.

12   Kathleen Elkins, "Amazon Will Pay HQ2 Employees an Average of $150,000—Here's How much Further That Goes in Nashville," CNBC, November 14, 2018, https://www.cnbc.com/2018/11/13/amazon-will-pay-hq2-employees-150000-dollars-that-goes-further-in-nashville.html.

13   "Mayor de Blasio and Governor Cuomo Announce Amazon Selects Long Island City for New Corporate Headquarters," New York City Mayor's Office, NYC.Gov, November 13, 2018, https://www.nyc.gov/office-of-the-mayor/news/552-18/mayor-de-blasio-governor-cuomo-amazon-selects-long-island-city-new-corporate#/0.

14   "2014 State and Local Primary Election Results," New York State Board of Elections Statewide Democratic Gubernatorial Primary, September 9, 2014, https://www.elections.ny.gov/NYSBOE/elections/2014/Primary/2014StateLocalPrimaryElectionResults.pdf; Ben Brachfeld, "A Closer Look at Voter Turnout in 2018 New York Congressional Primaries," Gotham Gazette, June 18, 2018, https://www.gothamgazette.com/state/7774-a-closer-look-at-voter-turnout-in-2018-new-york-congressional-primaries.

15   "Certified Results from the November 6, 2018 General Election for NYS Senate," New York State Board of Elections website, November 6, 2018, https://www.elections.ny.gov/NYSBOE/elections/2018/general/2018NYSenate.pdf.

16   "New York State Voter Enrollment by Senate District, Party Affiliation and Status: Voters Registered as of November 1, 2018," New York State Board of Elections website, accessed September 15, 2023, https://www.elections.ny.gov/NYSBOE/enrollment/senate/senate_nov18.xlsx; "Certified Results For Sept 13 Primary," New York State Board of Elections website, accessed September 15, 2013, https://www.elections.ny.gov/NYSBOE/elections/2018/Primary/CertifiedResultsForSept13Primary.xlsx.

17   Greg David, "NYC Lost a Record 631,000 Jobs to the Pandemic in 2020, So What's Next?," The City, March 14, 2021, https://www.thecity.nyc/economy/2021/3/14/22326414/nyc-lost-record-jobs-to-pandemic-unemployment.

18   Dennis Green and Walt Hickey, "Alexandria Ocasio-Cortez Says That $3 Billion in Tax Credits Should Be Given to the Public, not Amazon—and a New

Poll Shows That Nearly Half of Americans Agree," Business Insider, February 20, 2019, https://www.businessinsider.com/poll-most-dont-support-amazon-hq2-style-deal-2019-2.

19 Stephen Menedian et al., "The Most Segregated Cities and Neighborhoods in the San Francisco Bay Area: 2020 Census Update," Haas Institute for a Fair and Inclusive Society, University of California, Berkeley, October 11, 2021, https://belonging.berkeley.edu/most-segregated-cities-bay-area-2020.

20 J.K. Dineen, "Restrictive Zoning Keeps Marin the Most Segregated County in the Bay Area," *San Francisco Chronicle*, December 7, 2020, https://www.sfchronicle.com/bayarea/article/Restrictive-zoning-keeps-Marin-the-most-15782840.php.

21 Annie Lowrey, "Four Years Among the NIMBYs," *The Atlantic*, May 12, 2022, https://www.theatlantic.com/ideas/archive/2022/05/san-francisco-bureaucracy-housing-crisis/629719/.

22 Lowrey, "Four Years Among the NIMBYs."

23 "City of Chicago SD 299," U.S. News , accessed September 5, 2023, https://www.usnews.com/education/k12/illinois/districts/city-of-chicago-sd-299-110570.

24 "City of Chicago SD 299," U.S. News; Hannah Schmid, "Chicago Students Score Lower, Fewer Graduate, Fewer Go to College," *Illinois Policy*, Illinois Policy Institute, June 7, 2023, https://www.illinoispolicy.org/chicago-students-score-lower-fewer-graduate-fewer-go-to-college/.

25 Hannah Schmid, "One-Third of Chicago Public Schools Are Less Than Half Full," *Illinois Policy*, Illinois Policy Institute, June 28, 2023, https://www.illinoispolicy.org/one-third-of-chicago-public-schools-are-less-than-half-full.

26 Mailee Smith, "EP. 50: Why So Many Parents Are Leaving Chicago Public Schools," Illinois Policy, *Illinois Policy Institute*, August 24, 2022, https://www.illinoispolicy.org/policy-shop/ep-50-why-so-many-parents-are-leaving-chicago-public-schools/.

27 Shelby Mahaffie et al., "The Educational Attainment of Chicago Public Schools Students: 2021," University of Chicago Consortium on School Research, December 22, 2021, https://toandthrough.uchicago.edu/tool/cps/pai/2021/#.

28 "Mayor Brandon Johnson Biography," Chicago Public Library, accessed

September 14, 2023, https://www.chipublib.org/mayor-brandon-johnson -biography/.

29   Juan Perez Jr. and Shia Kapos, "'A Dangerous Force': Chicago Mayor's Race Tests Teachers Union Clout," Politico, April 3, 2023, https://www.politico .com/news/2023/04/03/teachers-union-chicago-mayor-runoff-00090022.

30   Matt Masterson and Erica Demarest, "'Slow and Sleepy' Chicago Voting Totals on Par with February Election Turnout," WTTW News, April 4, 2023, https://news.wttw.com/2023/04/04/slow-and-sleepy-chicago-voting-totals -par-february-election-turnout.

31   Sarah Schulte, "Did You Vote? Only 35% of Chicago Residents Turned Out to Vote in Runoff Election," ABC7 Chicago, April 6, 2023. https://abc7chicago .com/chicago-voter-turnout-2023-mayoral-election-voting-results-in /13096289/.

32   "Majority of Public Disapproves of Supreme Court's Decision to Overturn *Roe v. Wade*," Pew Research Center, July 6, 2022, https://www.pewresearch .org/politics/2022/07/06/majority-of-public-disapproves-of-supreme -courts-decision-to-overturn-roe-v-wade/.

33   "Americans' Views on Whether, and in What Circumstances, Abortion Should Be Legal," Pew Research Center, May 6, 2022, https://www .pewresearch.org/religion/2022/05/06/americans-views-on-whether-and -in-what-circumstances-abortion-should-be-legal/.

34   Differentiators Data, "School Nutrition Survey: Conducted February 28– March 2, 2023," accessed January 23, 2024, https://static1.squarespace .com/static/62f67867873052330581fb46/t/65aee9d81eee3f2304a7f568 /1705961947162/Polling+-+School+Hunger+Survey.pdf.

35   Prem Thakker, "Republicans Declare Banning Universal Free School Meals in 2024 a Priority." June 15, 2023, *New Republic*, https://newrepublic.com /post/173668/republicans-declare-banning-universal-free-school-meals -2024-priority.

36   Joshua Ferrer and Michael Thorning, "2022 Primary Turnout: Trends and Lessons for Boosting Participation Report," Bipartisan Policy Center, March 2023, 9, https://bipartisanpolicy.org/download/?file=/wp-content/uploads /2023/03/Primary-Turnout-Report_R03.pdf.

37   "Large Majorities of Voters Oppose Book Bans and Have Confidence in Libraries," American Library Association, March 24, 2022, https://www.ala

.org/news/press-releases/2022/03/large-majorities-voters-oppose-book
-bans-and-have-confidence-libraries.

38 *Wall Street Journal*, Baseline Nationwide Poll April 2023, April 11–17, 2023,
    https://s.wsj.net/public/resources/documents/WSJ_Poll_April_2023
    _redacted.pdf.

39 Kasey Meehan and Jonathan Friedman, "Update on Banned Books in the
    2022–2023 School Year Shows Expanded Censorship of Themes Centered
    on Race, History, Sexual Orientation and Gender," PEN America, April 20,
    2023,   https://pen.org/report/banned-in-the-usa-state-laws-supercharge
    -book-suppression-in-schools/.

40 Alexandra E. Petri, "Book Bans Are on the Rise in U.S. schools, Fueled by
    New Laws in Republican-Led States," *Los Angeles Times*, April 22, 2023,
    https://www.latimes.com/world-nation/story/2023-04-22/book-bans
    -soaring-schools-new-laws-republican-states.

41 "DSA Political Platform from 2021 Convention: Abolition of the Carceral
    State," Democratic Socialists of America, 2021, https://www.dsausa
    .org/dsa-political-platform-from-2021-convention/#abolition-carceral
    [Accessed September 15, 2023].

42 Linley Sanders, "What Police Reform Does America Support?," YouGov,
    June   1,   2020,   https://today.yougov.com/politics/articles/30003-police
    -reform-america-poll?

43 Gary Kamiya, "The Holier-Than-Thou Crusade in San Francisco," *The
    Atlantic*, February 2, 2021, https://www.theatlantic.com/ideas/archive/2021
    /02/san-francisco-renaming-spree/617894/.

CHAPTER 5

1   Data compiled from "Federal Voting Assistance Program 2020 Post-
    Election Report to Congress," Federal Voting Assistance Program, United
    States Government, 2020, accessed August 22, 2023, https://www.fvap.gov
    /info/reports-surveys/2020-report-to-congress and "State of the Military
    Voter," Federal Voting Assistance Program, United States Government,
    2020, accessed August 22, 2023, https://www.fvap.gov/info/reports-surveys
    /StateoftheMilitaryVoter.

2   "2020 Post-Election Report to Congress."

3   "Disability Impacts All of Us," Centers for Disease Control and Prevention.

Disability and Health Data System (DHDS), May 15, 2023, https://www.cdc
.gov/ncbddd/disabilityandhealth/infographic-disability-impacts-all.html.

4   Data compiled from "Voting and Registration in the Election of November
    2022," United States Census Bureau, April 2023, https://www.census.gov
    /data/tables/time-series/demo/voting-and-registration/p20–586.html.

5   "Disability Vote Grows to 38.3 Million, a 19.8% Jump Since 2008," *SMLR
    News*, Rutgers School of Management and Labor Relations, Rutgers
    University, September 25, 2020, https://smlr.rutgers.edu/news-events/smlr
    -news/disability-vote-grows-383-million-198-jump-2008.

6   "U.S. Election Assistance Commission Study on Disability and Voting
    Accessibility in the 2020 Elections," United States Election Assistance
    Commission, April 21, 2022, https://www.eac.gov/election-officials
    /us-election-assistance-commission-study-disability-and-voting
    -accessibility-2020.

7   "The Blind Voter Experience: A Comparison of the 2008, 2012, 2014, 2016,
    2018, and 2020 Elections," National Federation of the Blind, January 2021,
    https://nfb.org/sites/nfb.org/files/files-word/2020-Blind-Voter-Survey
    -Report.docx.

8   Matt Vasilogambros, "Voters with Disabilities Feel Left Behind by Paper
    Ballot Push," *Stateline*, September 18, 2019, https://stateline.org/2019/09/18
    /voters-with-disabilities-feel-left-behind-by-paper-ballot-push/.

9   Lisa Schur and Douglas Kruse, "Disability and Voting Accessibility in the
    2020 Elections: Final Report on Survey Results," U.S. Election Assistance
    Commission and Rutgers School of Management and Labor Relations,
    February 16, 2021, https://www.eac.gov/sites/default/files/voters/Disability
    _and_voting_accessibility_in_the_2020_elections_final_report_on_survey
    _results.pdf.

10 Lisa Schur and Douglas Kruse, "Fact Sheet: Disability and Voter Turnout
    in the 2016 Elections," Rutgers School of Management and Labor Relations,
    Rutgers University, accessed September 16, 2023, https://smlr.rutgers.edu
    /sites/default/files/Documents/Centers/Program_Disability_Research
    /Fact%20Sheet%20Disability%20Voter%202016%20Elections.pdf.

11 Schur and Kruse, "Disability and Voting Accessibility."

12 Sanya Mansoor, "They Have Lost So Much But They Will Not Lose Their
    Right to Vote.' Advocates Fight to Enfranchise Americans Displaced by

Wildfires," Time, September 25, 2020, https://time.com/5890215/wildfires
-displaced-voting/.

13   Kevin Morris and Peter Miller, "Hurricane Michael and the 2018 Elections,"
     Brennan Center for Justice, September 28, 2022, https://www.brennancenter
     .org/our-work/research-reports/hurricane-michael-and-2018-elections.

14   Andrew Briz et al., "Florida Governor Election Results 2018," Politico and
     Associated Press, accessed October 25, 2023, https://www.politico.com
     /election-results/2018/florida/governor/.

15   "Country Profile: United States Displacement Data," Internal Displacement
     Monitoring Centre, accessed October 25, 2023, https://www.internal
     -displacement.org/countries/united-states#displacement-data.

16   "Voting Rights for Native Americans," Library of Congress Classroom Materials
     on Elections, accessed September 27, 2023, https://www.loc.gov/classroom
     -materials/elections/right-to-vote/voting-rights-for-native-americans/.

17   James Thomas Tucker et al., *Obstacles at Every Turn: Barriers to Political
     Participation Faced by Native American Voters*, Native American Rights Fund,
     June 2020, accessed October 25, 2023, https://vote.narf.org/wp-content
     /uploads/2020/06/obstacles_at_every_turn.pdf.

18   Jean Schroedel et al., "Voting Barriers Encountered by Native Americans in
     Arizona, New Mexico, Nevada and South Dakota," Native American Voting
     Rights Coalition, January 2018, accessed October 25, 2023, https://www
     .narf.org/wordpress/wp-content/uploads/2018/01/2017NAVRCsurvey
     -summary.pdf; "American Indian and Alaska Native Heritage Month:
     November 2017," United States Census Newsroom, United States Census
     Bureau, October 6, 2017, https://www.census.gov/newsroom/facts-for
     -features/2017/aian-month.html.

19   "Access for Native Americans: Case Studies & Best Practices," U.S. Election
     Assistance Commission, November 10, 2021, https://www.eac.gov/sites
     /default/files/2021-11/Voting_Access_for_Native_Americans-Case_Studies
     _%26_Best_Practices.pdf .

20   "New Voting Restrictions in America," Brennan Center for Justice, last
     updated November 19, 2019, https://www.brennancenter.org/our-work
     /research-reports/new-voting-restrictions-america; "Shelby County v.
     Holder," Brennan Center for Justice, last updated June 25, 2023, https://www
     .brennancenter.org/our-work/court-cases/shelby-county-v-holder.

21 Amelia Thomson-DeVeaux et al., "Why Many Americans Don't Vote," FiveThirtyEight, October 26, 2020, https://projects.fivethirtyeight.com/non -voters-poll-2020-election/.

22 Mike Baker, "Rejected Mail Ballots Are Showing Racial Disparities," New York Times, February 2, 2022, https://www.nytimes.com/2022/02/02/us /mail-voting-black-latino.html.

23 Kevin Morris and Coryn Grange, "Records Show Massive Disenfranchisement and Racial Disparities in 2022 Texas Primary," Brennan Center for Justice, October 20, 2022, https://www.brennancenter.org/our-work/research -reports/records-show-massive-disenfranchisement-and-racial-disparities -2022-texas.

24 Kevin Morris and Coryn Grange, "Large Racial Turnout Gap Persisted in 2020 Election," Brennan Center for Justice, August 6, 2021, https://www .brennancenter.org/our-work/analysis-opinion/large-racial-turnout-gap -persisted-2020-election.

25 Jocelyn Benson et al., "Featured Session: Voting Is a Civil Rights Issue," taped March 13, 2023, in Austin, TX, SXSW Panel Recording, https://schedule .sxsw.com/2023/events/PP127666.

26 Sunshine Hillygus, "The Real Reason Young People Don't Vote," Issues in Science and Technology, October 20, 2020, https://issues.org/real-reason -young-people-dont-vote-hillygus/.

27 Matt Vasilogambros, "College Students Push to Ease Voting Access After Midterm Barriers," Stateline, November 18, 2022, https://stateline.org /2022/11/18/college-students-push-to-ease-voting-access-after-midterm -barriers/.

28 Statista, s.v. "U.S. Car Owners by Age Group," Statista Research Department, September 30, 2022, https://www.statista.com/statistics/1041145/us-car -owners-by-age-group/.

29 "Historical Reported Voting Rates," United States Census Bureau, last revised April 19, 2023, https://www.census.gov/data/tables/time-series/demo /voting-and-registration/voting-historical-time-series.html.

30 Elaine Kamarck and Alexander R. Podkul, "The 2018 Primaries Project: The Demographics of Primary Voters," Brookings Institute, October 23, 2018, https://www.brookings.edu/articles/the-2018-primaries-project-the -demographics-of-primary-voters/.

31 "Who Votes for Mayor," Portland State University, accessed August 4, 2023, http://whovotesformayor.org/.

CHAPTER 6

1   Chris Leaverton, "Who Controlled Redistricting in Every State?" Brennan Center for Justice, October 5, 2022, https://www.brennancenter.org/our -work/research-reports/who-controlled-redistricting-every-state.

2   Caroline Cournoyer, "Why It Will Likely Be Voters, Not Courts or Lawmakers, That Curb Partisan Gerrymandering," NBC News, October 21, 2019, https:// www.cbsnews.com/news/voters-supreme-court-lawmakers-partisan -gerrymandering-today-2019-10-21/.

3   Adam Edelman, "Big Year for States to Push for Ranked-Choice Voting," NBC News, January 16, 2023, https://www.nbcnews.com/politics/politics -news/big-year-states-push-ranked-choice-voting-rcna64945.

4   Jeffrey M. Jones, "U.S. Party Preferences Evenly Split in 2022, Shift to GOP," Gallup, January 12, 2023, https://news.gallup.com/poll/467897/party -preferences-evenly-split-2022-shift-gop.aspx.

5   "State Primary Election Types," National Conference of State Legislatures, accessed April 29th, https://www.ncsl.org/elections-and-campaigns/ state-primary-election-types#primaries.

6   Jeff Mapes, "Measure 90, Which Would Have Eliminated Partisan Primaries, Fails: Oregon Election Results 2014," OregonLive, November 5, 2014, https:// www.oregonlive.com/politics/2014/11/measure_90_which_would_have_el .html.

7   Jessica Hill, "Nevada's Largest Voting Bloc Can't Vote in a Primary. This Initiative Could Change That," Las Vegas Review-Journal, October 20, 2023, https://www.reviewjournal.com/news/politics-and-government/nevada /nevadas-largest-voting-bloc-cant-vote-in-a-primary-this-initiative-could -change-that-2925314/.

8   Miles Parks, "2020 Changed How America Votes. The Question Now Is Whether Those Changes Stick," NPR, October 28, 2022, https://www.npr.org /2022/10/28/1128695831/united-states-2022-patterns-mail-early-voting.

9   Jeffrey M. Jones, "Early Voting Higher Than in Past U.S. Midterms," Gallup, November 2, 2022, https://news.gallup.com/poll/404558/early-voting -higher-past-midterms.aspx.

10   Amber McReynolds and Charles Stewart III, "Opinion: Let's Put the Vote-by-Mail 'Fraud' Myth to Rest," *The Hill*, April 28, 2020, https://thehill.com /opinion/campaign/494189-lets-put-the-vote-by-mail-fraud-myth-to-rest/.

11   "Voting by Mail and Absentee Voting," MIT Election Data and Science Lab, last updated March 16, 2021, https://electionlab.mit.edu/research/voting -mail-and-absentee-voting.

12   Aidan Connaughton and Shannon Schumacher, "Many Western Europeans Think Mandatory Voting Is Important, But Americans Are Split," Pew Research Center, May 18, 2021, https://www.pewresearch.org/short -reads/2021/05/18/many-western-europeans-think-mandatory-voting-is -important-but-americans-are-split/.

13   Miles Rapoport and Janai S. Nelson, "Op-Ed: 2020 Election: What We Could Learn from Australia's Mandatory Voting," *Los Angeles Times*, August 20, 2020, https://www.latimes.com/opinion/story/2020-08-20/2020-election -mandatory-voting-australia.

14   Wikipedia, s.v. "Qualified New York Political Parties," last modified May 25, 2023, https://en.wikipedia.org/wiki/Qualified_New_York_political_parties.

CHAPTER 7

1   "Mobile Fact Sheet," Pew Research Center, April 7, 2021, https://www .pewresearch.org/internet/fact-sheet/mobile/.

2   Natasha Lomas, "Don't Break Regulation—Get a Policy Strategy Now, Startups Told," TechCrunch, September 14, 2016, https://techcrunch.com /2016/09/14/dont-break-regulation-get-a-policy-strategy-now-startups -told/.

3   Tomicah Tillemann et al., "The Blueprint for Blockchain and Social Innovation, Case Studies," Blockchain Trust Accelerator, New America, last updated January 22, 2019, https://www.newamerica.org/digital-impact -governance-initiative/blockchain-trust-accelerator/reports/blueprint -blockchain-and-social-innovation/case-studies/#voting-west-virginia.

4   Larry Moore and Nimit Sawhney, "Under The Hood: The West Virginia Mobile Voting Pilot," Voatz, January 20, 2019, https://www.nass.org/sites /default/files/2019–02/white-paper-voatz-nass-winter19.pdf.

5   "Enhanced Security and Access for UOCAVA Voters: Denver Elections Division, CO," Election Center, accessed January 20, 2024, https://www.electioncenter

.org/national-association-of-election-officials/election-adminstration-and
-voter-registration/professional-practice-papers/2019/35th-Annual-National
-Conference-Orlando-Florida/Democracy-Award/Outstanding-Practice-Of
-2019/Enhanced-Security-and-Access-for-UOCAVA-Voters-Bucaro-Miller
-Denver-Elections-Division-Colorado.pdf; "The Denver Mobile Voting Pilot:
A Report," Mobile Voting, accessed February 1, 2024, https://mobilevoting.org
/resources/the-denver-mobile-voting-pilot-a-report/.

CHAPTER 8

1   "Cast-as-Intended Verifiability," Karlsruhe Institute of Technology, accessed
January 30, 2024, https://secuso.aifb.kit.edu/english/943.php; Josh Benaloh
et al., *End-to-end Verifiability* (University of California, Berkeley 2015),
https://escholarship.org/content/qt7c9994dg/qt7c9994dg.pdf.

2   Katherine M. Jia et al., "Estimated Preventable COVID-19-Associated
Deaths Due to Non-Vaccination in the United States," *European Journal of
Epidemiology* 38, no. 11 (April 2023): 1125, https://www.ncbi.nlm.nih.gov
/pmc/articles/PMC10123459/.

3   Zachary Laub et al., "A Timeline of the Iraq War," PBS NewsHour, March 7,
2023, https://www.pbs.org/newshour/world/a-timeline-of-the-iraq-war.

4   "Timeline of the Iraq War."

5   Charles P. Pierce, "15 Years. More Than 1 Million Dead. No One Held
Responsible," *Esquire*, March 21, 2018, https://www.esquire.com/news
-politics/politics/a19547603/iraq-15-years-george-bush/.

6   "Immediate Release: Casualty Status," United States Department of Defense,
October 16, 2023, https://www.defense.gov/casualty.pdf.

7   Neta C. Crawford, "US Budgetary Costs of Wars through 2016: $4.79 Trillion
and Counting," Watson Institute for International and Public Affairs at Brown
University, September 2016, https://watson.brown.edu/costsofwar/files/cow
/imce/papers/2016/Costs%20of%20War%20through%202016%20FINAL
%20final%20v2.pdf.

8   *The 9/11 Commission Report* (Washington, DC: National Commission on
Terrorist Attacks, 2004), https://9–11commission.gov/report/.

9   "Who We Are," Verified Voting, accessed January 5, 2024, https://
verifiedvoting.org/team/.

CHAPTER 9

1   U.S. Vote Foundation, "The Future of Voting: End-to-End Verifiable Internet Voting—Specification and Feasibility Study," accessed January 21, 2024, https://www.usvotefoundation.org/E2E-VIV.

2   Susan Greenhalgh et al., *Email and Internet Voting: The Overlooked Threat to Election Security*, Common Cause, 2020, https://www.commoncause.org/ wp-content/uploads/2018/10/ElectionSecurityReport.pdf.

3   Nate Cohn and Kevin Quealy, "A Mysterious 'Undervote' Could End Up Settling the Florida Senate Race," *New York Times*, November 9, 2018, https://www.nytimes .com/2018/11/09/upshot/florida-senate-race-broward-undercount.html.

4   Data compiled from "Federal Voting Assistance Program 2020 Post-Election Report to Congress," Federal Voting Assistance Program, United States Government, 2020, accessed August 22, 2023, https://www.fvap.gov/info/reports -surveys/2020-report-to-congress, and "State of the Military Voter" Federal Voting Assistance Program, United States Government, 2020, accessed August 22, 2023, https://www.fvap.gov/info/reports-surveys/StateoftheMilitaryVoter.

CHAPTER 10

1   Tyler Clifford, "'Life Is Wild!' First Generation Z Member Elected to U.S. Congress," Reuters, November 9, 2022, https://www.reuters.com /world/us/life-is-wild-first-generation-z-member-elected-us-congress -2022-11-09/; Juliana Kaplan, "The Oldest Gen Alphas Can Almost Drive: Here's How Millennials' Kids Will Shop, Work, and Live," Business Insider, January 16, 2024, https://www.businessinsider.com /who-is-generation-alpha-how-shop-spend-education-work-live-2024-1..

2   Jenna McNamee, "Banks Must Turn to Digital and Mobile to Capture the Hearts of Gen Z," Insider Intelligence, March 1, 2023, https://www.insiderintelligence .com/content/banks-must-turn-digital-mobile-capture-hearts-of-gen-z.

3   "The Mobile-First Generation: Gen Z Is Heavily into Mobile Gaming, Shopping, and Social Media, Finds Tapjoy's New Modern Mobile Gamer Report," *Ad Tech Daily*, June 17, 2021, adtechdaily.com/2021/06 /17/the-mobile-first-generation-gen-z-is-heavily-into-mobile-gaming -shopping-and-social-media-finds-tapjoys-new-modern-mobile-gamer -report/.

4   Victoria Petrock, "US Generation Z Technology and Media Use," Insider

Intelligence, November 15, 2021, www.insiderintelligence.com/content/us
-generation-z-technology-and-media-use#page-report.

5   Statista, s.v. "Internet Usage Worldwide," accessed September 4, 2023, https://
www.statista.com/study/12322/global-internet-usage-statista-dossier/.

6   Emily A. Vogels et al., "Teens, Social Media and Technology 2022," Pew
Research Center, August 10, 2022, https://www.pewresearch.org/internet
/2022/08/10/teens-social-media-and-technology-2022/.

7   Kyler Alvord, "Maxwell Frost, Gen Z's First Member of Congress on Breaking
Barriers, Couch Surfing and 'M3GAN,'" People, January 25, 2023, https://
people.com/politics/maxwell-frost-gen-z-congressman-breaking-barriers.

8   Carrie Blazina and Drew Desilver, "House Gets Younger, Senate Gets Older:
A Look at the Age and Generation of Lawmakers in the 118th Congress,"
Pew Research Center, January 30, 2023, https://www.pewresearch.org/short
-reads/2023/01/30/house-gets-younger-senate-gets-older-a-look-at-the
-age-and-generation-of-lawmakers-in-the-118th-congress/.

9   "The Gun Violence Prevention Movement Fueled Youth Engagement in
2018," Tufts University, Tisch College of Civic Life, February 15, 2019,
https://circle.tufts.edu/latest-research/gun-violence-prevention-movement
-fueled-youth-engagement-2018-election.

10 Maria Perez, "Laura Ingraham Advertising Boycott: Htwere Are the Companies
That Have Pulled Out of Fox News Host's Show," Newsweek, April 6, 2018, https://
www.newsweek.com/laura-ingraham-david-hogg-advertisements-875876.

11 Kurzman, Charles. "The Arab Spring: Ideals of the Iranian Green Movement,
Methods of the Iranian Revolution." International Journal of Middle East Studies
44, no. 1 (February 2012): 162. http://www.jstor.org/stable/41474990.

12 Farnaz Fassihi, "How Two Teenagers Became the New Faces of Iran's
Protests," New York Times, October 3, 2022, https://www.nytimes.com/2022
/10/13/world/middleeast/iran-protests-killed-teens.html.

13 Rick Rojas, "An Ailing Arkansas City Elected an 18-Year-Old Mayor to Turn
Things Around." New York Times, January 10, 2023, https://www.nytimes
.com/2023/01/10/us/jaylen-smith-mayor-earle-arkansas.html.

14 Chloe Malle, "Inside the Sunrise Movement: Six Weeks with the Young Activists
Defining the Climate Debate," Vogue, September 20, 2019, https://www.vogue
.com/article/inside-sunrise-movement-youth-activists-climate-debate.

15 "H.Res.109—116th Congress (2019–2020): Recognizing the Duty of the

Federal Government to Create a Green New Deal," House Resolution 109, 116th Congress (2019), https://www.congress.gov/bill/116th-congress/house-resolution/109.

16 Jesse D. Jenkins et al., "Preliminary Report: The Climate and Energy Impacts of the Inflation Reduction Act of 2022," REPEAT (Reconciliation for Environmental Progress, Equity, and Transformation) Project, Zero Lab, Princeton University, August 4, 2022, https://repeatproject.org/docs/REPEAT_IRA_Prelminary_Report_2022-08-04.pdf.

17 Ellis Juhlin, "A Decision Will Soon Be Made in the Nation's First Youth-Led Climate Lawsuit," NPR, June 25, 2023, https://www.npr.org/2023/06/25/1184198876/a-decision-will-soon-be-made-in-the-nations-first-youth-led-climate-lawsuit.

18 Jeffrey Kluger, "Kids Just Brought Montana to Court over Climate Change. The Case Could Make Waves beyond the State." *Time*, June 23, 2023, https://time.com/6289898/montana-climate-lawsuit-us/.

19 Kate Selig, "Youths Sued Montana over Climate Change and Won," *Washington Post*, August 16, 2023, https://www.washingtonpost.com/climate-environment/2023/08/17/montana-climate-lawsuit-impact/.

20 "*Juliana v. United States*." Our Children's Trust, accessed September 5, 2023, https://www.ourchildrenstrust.org/juliana-v-us.

21 Alec Tyson et al., "Gen Z, Millennials Stand Out for Climate Change Activism, Social Media Engagement with Issue." Pew Research Center, May 26, 2021, https://www.pewresearch.org/science/2021/05/26/gen-z-millennials-stand-out-for-climate-change-activism-social-media-engagement-with-issue/.

22 Libby Stanford, "Gen Z Has a Passion for Political Activism. Schools Can Nurture It." *Education Week*, January 6, 2023, https://www.edweek.org/teaching-learning/gen-z-has-a-passion-for-political-activism-schools-can-nurture-it/2023/01.

APPENDIX 2

1 "Summary: Electronic Ballot Return," National Conference of State Legislatures, last updated January 19, 2023, https://www.ncsl.org/elections-and-campaigns/electronic-ballot-return-internet-voting.

2 "Comparative Risk Analysis of the Current UOCAVA Voting System and an Electronic Alternative," Federal Voting Assistance Program, Federal Voting

Assistance Program (FVAP) Technology Projects, February 2013, https://www
.fvap.gov/uploads/FVAP/ComparativeRiskAnalysisReport_20151228.pdf.

APPENDIX 3

1   "Comparative Risk Analysis of the Current UOCAVA Voting System and an
     Electronic Alternative," Federal Voting Assistance Program, February 2013, Page
     78,   https://www.fvap.gov/uploads/FVAP/ComparativeRiskAnalysisReport
     _20151228.pdf.

2   "New Data: 17.7 Million Americans with Disabilities Voted in 2020, a
     Significant Increase over 2016," Election Assistance Commission, July 7, 2021,
     https://www.eac.gov/news/2021/07/07/new-data-177-million-americans
     -disabilities-voted-2020-significant-increase-over.

3   "Comparative Risk Analysis of the Current UOCAVA Voting System."

ABOUT THE AUTHOR

Bradley Tusk is a venture capitalist, political strategist, philanthropist, and writer.

He is the CEO and cofounder of Tusk Ventures, the world's first venture capital fund that invests solely in early-stage startups in highly regulated industries, and the founder of political consulting firm Tusk Strategies. Bradley's family foundation is funding and leading the national campaign to bring mobile voting to all U.S. elections. Tusk Philanthropies also runs and funds anti-hunger campaigns that have led to the creation of anti-hunger policies and programs (including universal school breakfast programs) in nineteen different states, helping to feed more than 13 million people and counting.

Bradley is the author of *The Fixer: My Adventures Saving Startups from Death by Politics* and the novel *Obvious in Hindsight*, writes a column for the New York Daily News, hosts a podcast called Firewall about the intersection of tech and politics, and is cofounder of the Gotham Book Prize. He owns a bookstore, podcast studio, event space, and cafe called P&T Knitwear on Manhattan's Lower East Side. He is also an adjunct professor at Columbia Business School.

Previously, Bradley served as campaign manager for Mike Bloomberg's 2009 mayoral race, as deputy governor of Illinois, overseeing the state's budget, operations, legislation, policy, and communications, as communications director for U.S. Senator Chuck Schumer, and as Uber's first political advisor.